D1002523

Strap on your Boots

A realistic guide to building and scaling your startup

By

Jason Sherman

Copyright, Legal Notice and Disclaimer:

Any trademarks, service marks, product names or named features are assumed to be the property of their respective owners, and are used only for reference. There is no implied endorsement if we use one of these terms.

Published by Bootstrap Books

ISBN-13: 978-0692790427

I would like to dedicate this book to my parents:
Marc and Gloria Sherman,
who have given me the most amazing life a guy could ask for. Without their support, I wouldn't be where I am today. I will always love you both, in this life and the next.

I'd also like to dedicate this book to God, my family and supportive friends, and to anyone I've ever done business with. Lastly, I would like to give a fist bump to entrepreneurs and business owners out there who execute on their great ideas and, like me, are making the world a better place one day at a time.

CHAPTERS

Introduction

I would like to begin this book by saying that I'm not a millionaire. I want to make this clear because most books about starting a business are written by millionaires who make you think that you too can become a millionaire if you follow their instructions. I'm here to tell you that, in most cases, that's just not true. These millionaires tell their very situational success stories that are often difficult to duplicate. In terms of inspiration, those books definitely help boost your morale and give you a glimpse of hope. In terms of actual realistic expectations, well that's another story. If you've ever been told "no", I'm here to tell you that you can get a "yes". If you've ever been frustrated and wanted to give up, I assure you that there is another path you can take. If you've ever wondered how to truly start your own company, I will tell you how to do just that.

I have two reasons for writing this book. The first is to help entrepreneurs like yourself save a few years of time, money, mistakes, and stress. The second is to teach you how to realistically build and scale your startup, whether it be hardware, software, or otherwise. I may not be a millionaire, but based on my experience and personal success I sure feel like one. Sure, I've made a million dollars over the course of my entire career, but I am not wealthy. Comfortable yes, wealthy no. What is success really? Is it how much money you have in the bank, or how many things you own? To some maybe it is. But to me, it is one thing, and one thing only: Freedom. I have been a full time self-employed entrepreneur since 2005, meaning I haven't held a corporate job (or any job) with a paycheck since then. I have started many companies, and earned a decent income as a result of hard work, research, and passion. I have never struggled to buy something I wanted, and have lived every second of my life as if it was the most amazing gift given to me.

I'm not going to tell you that you can do the same thing I have done. As a matter of fact, I'm going to tell you that maybe you shouldn't even try. Why? Because starting your own company will be the hardest thing you will ever have to do in your life. Most people are happy (or so they say), with a full time corporate job, family, home, and that's it. Starting a new company can be just as hard as raising a child. If you have a child, you know how difficult it is. You have to nurture it, raise it, help it grow, and give it a tremendous amount of attention. So if you aren't ready to add another kid to your pack, then close this book, and hand it to someone who is ready.

However, if you like a challenge, then I dare you to continue reading...

Ideation

So you made it this far. That means you have an idea that is poking around in your mind. Well, I'm sorry to tell you that the age old saying, *"Ideas are a dime a dozen"* is true. It's all about using a unique perspective to differentiate your idea from others. What most experts will tell you is that the best ideas come out of a personal problem you are trying to solve. Sure, there are innovations like the iPhone that don't really solve a problem, but they make life easier and more productive (except when you're watching cat videos). For the most part, solving a problem that you currently face is the best way to start a new company.

The next piece of solving a problem is whether or not this is a problem other people also face. For example, let's say you lose your socks often and want to build a new sock drawer organizer. Will other people use it, or will they just keep throwing their socks in a drawer and put up with the occasional lost sock? My point is, your idea has to be compelling enough that people will actually care enough to buy or use your product. So you are probably asking me, "How will I know if people will care about my product?" Good question. Before you will know the answer, you have to find a solution to your problem first. You can't just say that you are building a new mobile app that helps you find your lost socks. You need to find out what people actually want in a mobile app that helps them find their lost socks.

There's a big difference in what you think people want, and what they actually want.

Vetting your idea is one of the most crucial moments in the ideation process. For example, what kind of characteristics of socks can this app find? Colored? White? Decorative? Costume? Size? Material? Age? Sentimental Value?

I'll bet you didn't think that socks had that many variables. Scientists have even come up with a 'Sock Loss Index[1],' which is: $(L(p \times f) + C(t \times s)) - (P \times A)$. Maybe you can use this formula in your mobile app to develop an algorithm that helps people lose less socks. Just something to think about. Now you might ask yourself, *"Why did Jason choose socks for his first example?."* Easy answer. Because (almost) everybody wears socks in the developed world. Choosing a problem to solve should have a high point of penetration in the market. If, instead of building a sock-finding app, maybe your idea has to do with determining what time it is based on your dog's sleeping habits. Maybe people will use it, maybe they won't. Your idea will have a higher likelihood of success if you solve a problem that affects a large part of the world's population.

---

[1] http://socks.jasonsherman.org

9

As for why I chose socks for my example, well you can't strap on your boots without putting on your socks first! To vet your idea, the first thing you have to do is ask your friends and family what they think of the idea. This way you will not only get initial feedback, but possibly great suggestions that will make your idea better. Once you get enough positive feedback that makes you feel comfortable to continue, it's time to create a short survey (I like to use Typeform.com) to get answers from the public. This way you can get unbiased feedback from complete strangers. You want to keep the survey short, and use multiple choice questions for speed. Always ask for an email address at the end of your survey so that you can send out a newsletter or a Beta invite email. Most entrepreneurs fail to create and send out a survey before starting a new company. This is a big mistake.

Why in the world would you spend six months to a year (or more) building a new mobile app when you haven't even asked people if they would use it? Creating a survey might take you an hour at the most, and sending it out to people another few hours. What's better, wasting a few hours or a few months (or years)? You know the answer.

The best part about a survey is that you may get data regarding your idea that you didn't previously think was important. Usually, this data ends up being instrumental in your success. For example, if you are building a video curation app, the results you get in this multiple choice question may cause you to rethink your initial reasoning behind the idea:

What type of videos would you curate in our mobile app?

*Choose as many as you like

a Comedy	b Science	c Pets	d Music
e News	f Sports	g Movies	h How to
i Other			

If an excessively high percentage of survey respondents answer A) Comedy or C) Pets, then maybe you should create a niche mobile app that only curates comedy or pet videos (or both) because you know there is a market for it. Don't worry, you can always open the app up to other genres later. It's always smart to solidify your place in the market with a guaranteed user base of people who have shown an interest in your particular niche.

In my opinion, the top five most important questions you will want to ask in your survey are:

1. Age of respondent
2. Their interest in your platform
3. The features they most want to use
4. How much they would pay for those features
5. Their email address

Any other questions you add are called "fluff," and you don't necessarily need them (although you might think you do). Most people don't like taking surveys, so the shorter and simpler it is, the more likely you are going to get a ton of responses. Then, based on the answers, you will have a better idea what people think of your initial idea. Plus, with their email addresses you can follow up later on to get more information from them via a newsletter, second survey, Beta launch invite, etc.

What I am trying to teach you in this book is to focus on the things you can control. Yes, you will have to put in a decent amount of effort initially, but if you focus on the things you can control, you will succeed no matter what. Even if your product never makes any money, or only gets 100 users, you will have learned the right way to do things, and the next time it will be that much easier. In the Star Wars universe, if Master Jedi Yoda was a tech entrepreneur he would have said, *"No failure there is. Only learning."* As for things you can't control, the biggest one is: Timing.

Timing is one of the most considerable wildcard factors in a new startup. I can't tell you how many times I have witnessed friends lose hundreds of thousands of dollars on a new venture because of timing. You might have the most revolutionary product in the world, but if you launch it at the wrong time, nobody is going to care. Timing is completely uncontrollable. All you can do is carefully vet your idea to make sure there is a market for it and then do everything in your power to let the world know that it exists. An effective way to find out if the timing is right for your idea is to do market research. Have others attempted your idea in the past? If so, did they succeed? If not, what happened? Do you have any current competitors? If so, how are they doing?

One of the ways that I do research is by reading news articles. My news reader of choice is Flipboard because I love their UI (User Interface) & UX (User Experience). It's simple, easy to use, and I can read a ton of articles in a short amount of time. You want to focus on your space (the marketable area in which your idea is positioned) and read articles that are related to your idea. For example, if you are building a new music collaboration platform, then you will want to read anything and everything related to the music technology industry. So anytime a new music app launches, gets funding, becomes acquired, gets buzz, or a celebrity endorses it, your job is to find out why. Ask yourself a few questions:

- What is so compelling about this app?
- What is their user engagement like?
- What's the background on the founders?
- Who invested in it?
- What is the UI / UX like?
- What is their core value proposition?
- How do they monetize?

You can also ask yourself many other questions. The more answers you get, the better you will understand your space and how to position your platform to differentiate yourself from the others. Before you move forward with truly building your company, you should understand your space inside and out. You can also use ProductHunt.com to find unique new companies that are popping up every day. This is another form of research: not just learning about successful companies, but finding out about new ones. Who knows, you might discover that your exact same idea has already launched. You just have to do enough digging to cover all of your bases.

Again, you might think your idea is incredible, but without substantive data to back it up, you might be heading for a black hole of doom. So make sure the timing is right. In the worst case scenario, you can do some research, create a survey, gather some data, and then let the idea sit on the back burner until the time is right. There's no shame in ideating with the eventual goal of creating the product (unless someone else does it first). For example, I had an idea for an app that allowed fellow entrepreneurs to vet an idea and collaborate together on the idea. I created mockups, diagrams, and documentation, but let the idea sit because I felt as though it wasn't the right time. Four years later GoDaddy Inc. launched an identical app[2]. Just goes to show you, the idea was spot on, but the timing was off by four years. Will I ever know if building the app four years

_____

[2]http://jasonsherman.org/godaddy

ago would have worked out? Of course not, but at least I have a vague idea that the concept may have been four years too early for the market. Kicking myself over it is a moot point; instead, I feel validated by a billion dollar company for having created a platform that I came up with four years before they launched it. Again, success comes in many forms. Validation is one of them.

Once you have determined that the time is right to launch your new product, using the data you received from the survey, you can ensure that it hits your target market. Making decisions based on data is one of the key pieces that has driven my success over the years. You may think you know it all, but trust me, you don't. The market knows better than you do. Also, being first to market isn't always necessarily a good thing. You might think, *"No one has ever done this before, I'm gonna take over the world!"* But without any market data, how do you know if that's true? Sometimes it's better to improve upon an existing idea to make it better, and base your decisions on data rather than what you think is a good idea.

As the late Steve Jobs once said, *"You don't have to be the first, but you've got to be the best."*

Take Myspace for example. In 2005, they were acquired by News Corporation for $580 million. Then Facebook launched, and well, you know what happened next. Myspace may have been the first, although some will argue AOL and Friendster were first. But Facebook made a better product and everyone flocked to the new and exclusive platform. This scenario has happened many times over the past century, and will continue to happen for the next few centuries. Will you be a part of that trend, or will you break through with something unique? That's up to you to decide. Just make sure you prepare yourself with data before you take the leap.

Now that you know using data to drive your decisions is of the utmost importance, you might be wondering how you actually do it. Personally, I look to answer a few questions in order to make my decisions. Here are some of them:

1. What is my target market?
2. What is my core value proposition?
3. How will I monetize?
4. What is the best way to engage my users?

There are plenty of other questions I can ask, but to get you started, these are the most important. Let's tackle each one together. To find your target market, first you will use the data from your survey. Hopefully you included a question about age. Age is one of the single most important pieces of information to discover your target market. Kids? Tweens? Millennials? College Grads? Middle-aged professionals? Baby Boomers? Elderly? Once you know this, then you will want to break down some other numbers that you have gathered from your websites' analytics. If you are saying, *"Wait, I don't have any analytics on my website,"* Then now is the time to get some on there. All it takes is for you to sign up for Google Analytics (G.A.), and drop a line of code onto each page you want to get some analytics from. It's free to use, and gives you some powerful data.

Now that you have G.A. on your website, you will be able to not only see age groups, but also:

- Demographics
- Location
- Browser & device type
- Last page visited
- Keywords used
- Conversion rates
- New and returning visitors
- Page views

There are so many more pieces of data you can get from G.A.; these are just some of them. You should be able to determine which pieces of data you need the most depending on what your product is. For example, maybe your product is a new bluetooth enabled running shoe. You want to build a prototype, but before you spend the time and money building it, you want to make sure people will actually want to pre-order it on Kickstarter. So here's what you do.

Using your survey data and your G.A. data you will have an idea who your target market is. Now you want to target those people who are interested in pre-ordering your product. Based on your data, you might find out that the target is a 22 to 34 year old who has an income of at least $50,000 a year, a gym membership, lives within a 50 mile radius of New York City, and is currently single. This means that when you spend a little bit of money on Facebook ads to promote your product, you know exactly what parameters to enter into your ad. I would think $50 should suffice. Make sure you have a way to accept pre-orders on your website. A PayPal checkout is easiest, but you might want to customize your user experience using Stripe or some other payment processor to make your site seem a bit more professional. See how many people pre-order your product. Try to get as many sales as you need, minus advertising expenses, in order to pay for the supplies to build your prototype.

If you have succeeded, then you have officially started your business and congratulations are in order! If you have not succeeded, don't give up just yet. You might just need more time. Patience is also a very important factor in the difference between succeeding and failing (learning). Patience, unlike timing, is something you can control. Sometimes you need more time and sometimes you don't; there are many variables that determine when it's time to pivot or throw in the towel. I'll cover that later. For now, you want to focus on your target market, and make sure you reach them properly. You can also take things a step further by going to the places they frequent. In this case you know they go to a gym, so maybe you can talk to the owners at your local gym and see if they would like to partner up with you on your new bluetooth enabled running shoe. Tell them that they can earn a commission on every pre-order that comes from their gym.

To do this you will need two things. First, a simple flyer unique to their gym explaining what the product is. The second is a trackable link on the flyer that people will use to go to your site and pre-order your product. What I do is create a URL forwarder that goes to a Bit.ly link connecting to a unique pre-order page you made for that gym. If you aren't sure how to do that, it's quite simple. First, on your domain hosting control panel, you will create a URL forwarder. Let's say you are calling the shoe, 'Blue-Shoe', and your domain is http://BlueShoe.com. Just create a URL forwarder with a simple and easily recognizable name such as http://GymName.Blueshoe.com and have that redirect to your http://Bit.ly link, and have that link go to the custom pre-order page you made for that gym. You can create as many of these as you want, and each one is trackable in Bit.ly so you can see how many people have clicked on that link.

You can also create URL's for other pages like: http://Survey.BlueShoe.com that goes to your Typeform

URL, which will be something a little less user friendly: https://blueshoe.typeform.com/to/bdnvlw. With custom URLs you will always remember what page to give to people, which will help them remember it also.

Then, using G.A., you can get more data on your purchases so that you know where they came from. Alternatively, you can also enable ecommerce reporting in G.A. under your main website profile. The best part is, all of this is free to do. There are many ways you can do this; I'm just giving you one example. Use your creativity to spark an interest in your target market and get pre-orders for your product or beta signups for your mobile app. Using the data from your analytics you can put together a spreadsheet with multiple worksheets. I've built many of these over the years with the help of my various teams. One spreadsheet in particular was so good that it has been used by tech accelerators as a template. The most common way to determine certain metrics for your company is by using what's called a customer acquisition funnel.

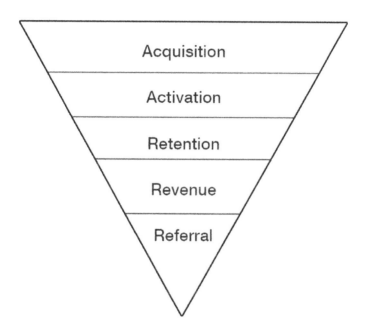

This "top-down" funnel keeps track of a few things:

- Acquisitions (how many people came to your site)
- Activations (how many people signed up to your platform)
- Retention (how many people came back to use your platform again)
- Revenue (people who paid for something on your platform)
- Referrals (where they came from)

You can keep track of other numbers too, but these are pretty much the most important ones. This should be a weekly thing, and you should be constantly updating and understanding these numbers, since they will be helping you make decisions. I always keep track of these numbers daily, weekly, and monthly. My goal is always to obtain highly specific numbers. You might also want to include other metrics in your spreadsheet separate from your funnel such as:

- Marketing campaign breakdown
- Daily, weekly & monthly downloads
- Daily, weekly & monthly installs
- DAU (Daily Active Users) & MAU (Monthly Active Users)
- Gender & age
- Device & location

These and many other important metrics (such as user engagement stats), have always helped me make important decisions about the path I should take moving forward. If you are still wondering how the funnel works, it's quite simple. It works like any other funnel. For example, if you are going to put oil in your car, you pour it into a funnel. If something is blocking the bottom, the oil won't reach your oil tank. The same goes for the acquisition funnel. Let's say something is blocking retention. This means that you are able to get visitors to your website, and even get them to sign up. But for some reason they aren't coming back to use it again. Something is obviously wrong.

How do you unblock the funnel? Well, first you have to find out what is causing the blockage. What is the last thing visitors are doing on your website? G.A. should provide some insight into this. You can also use a heat map system like CrazyEgg.com to find out exactly where your visitors were before they went away. Once you figure out what is causing them to leave, you can fix the problem, and see if your funnel starts to trickle down past retention onto revenue. Here are a few examples of what could be wrong in a variety of platforms.

On your crowd sourcing, video, news platform, your video uploading feature was taking too long. Maybe you didn't have enough users to be matched with on your dating site. It could be that the contractors on your dog walking platform didn't have a background check. Maybe your profile creation process was just too cumbersome for your job seeking platform. Whatever the issue, once you fix it, you will be able to send out an email using Mailchimp.com to your userbase to let them know that you have fixed the problem, and would like to see what they think of the platform now.

Keep in mind, this works for any piece of the funnel. Why aren't your users paying for any of your features? Or why aren't they purchasing a particular upgrade you thought was important? Why aren't they signing up for your platform? Why are they only coming back once a month instead of once a week? These are some of the questions you might end up asking yourself by using the funnel.

By keeping track of your data and analyzing the results, you are finding out whether or not people like your idea. Essentially, you are trying to gauge the interest on your core value proposition. Your "value prop" is the main reason people will want to use your product.

What value does my product add to a person's life?

The mistake most entrepreneurs make when building a new software platform is that they don't concentrate on one core feature. Often when I help a new startup they always say, *"My idea will give Facebook (or some other behemoth), a run for their money."* This is hardly ever the case; in fact it's pretty rare. There is a great infographic on Mashable[3] that shows a pretty detailed breakdown on the success rate of startups. The numbers are staggering. Out of all the numbers, by far the most eye-opening is that only 18% of entrepreneurs succeed in their first venture. That means that you are probably one of the 82% that will fail in your startup. Once you accept that fact, you will enjoy the journey much more and focus on building your product instead of concentrating on the final outcome.

One way you can get into the elite 18% of successful entrepreneurs is to focus on one core feature and use my methodologies to test that feature in the market. For example, one of my earlier tech startups was a social commerce platform that simply didn't exist. It was 2009 and the only real contenders were eBay and Craigslist. There were a handful of new mobile apps popping up that were basically hyper-local versions of Craigslist. Some got funding, and some didn't. Where my idea stood out was that my team and I incorporated little bits and pieces of what worked well in other platforms. For example, on our platform you had a real profile (like Facebook) and the ability to instantly chat with members. You could also add videos showcasing your products for sale. We had a Pinterest-style 'For Sale' page where you could list anything for free. We only took a small commission if you sold something. We also had a ton of other features. We

---

[3] http://mashable.jasonsherman.org

built this huge platform and actually found out that people liked what we offered.

Unfortunately, marketing such a detailed platform was difficult to do (and expensive), mostly because we hadn't done the research first. We just knew that our platform was more social, less prone to scams, more interactive, easier to use, and very community oriented. Interestingly enough, our users ended up bartering with each other on their sale prices via instant chat or our user forums. So we had an idea. We would let buyers dictate the price they are willing to spend on an item, and allow sellers to "match the price" if they had that item in stock. If the buyer and seller were matched, they would be engaged in a sale, and could instantly chat to figure out the details of the purchase. After finding all of this out, we built a payment and shipping system into the platform so they could finalize the sale right then and there.

Ultimately our core value prop ended up being a "reverse auction" system where the buyers dictated the price. If only we had known this from the beginning, we wouldn't have spent a year or longer building the behemoth of a social commerce platform that we ended up building. We could have just built the simplistic reverse auction feed that we featured on our homepage when we ran out of money and when two of the founders left the company. Suffice it to say, we dissolved the company and parted ways. My partners obviously didn't have the patience to continue. That's the last time I have built a platform without first validating a core value proposition using the methods I have already explained.

Once you determine the single most valuable function or feature, you will want to iterate upon that feature until you have almost perfected it. Iteration is done by building your core feature, testing it with your beta users, gathering data, making a decision, and then changing your product in small increments. You do this over and over again in short amounts of time until your value prop is exactly what your target market is looking for. Just remember, you want to constantly be testing your value prop with actual people, not just friends and family. You should always have a pool of beta testers, and continue to grow that pool while iterating. By doing this, you are essentially growing your userbase slowly while gathering crucial data.

Once you have grown your userbase and gathered useful data, you will want to monetize your users. Monetization means implementing revenue streams in one or more of your features. For example, if your new mobile app lets people find the dessert shops that are closest to their GPS location, you can monetize by charging shops a monthly fee for being on the app. Or you could offer coupons on the app for people to use, and every time they redeem a coupon, the shop pays you a 10% commission for getting them in the door. There are many ways to monetize your products; you just have to be creative when you do.

It's easy for a tech startup founder to say, *"I'm just going to put ads in my mobile app."* That's not very creative though. Besides, ads don't work if you don't have a large userbase, so you will just annoy the users you do have with ads, and they will most likely stop using your platform altogether. So with monetization, you have to truly think outside the box. Besides your value prop, what is it that will drive people to use your app over and over again? That feature or function is what you will be able to monetize. Maybe it's a monthly fee to be a member, or buying credits to upgrade their avatar in your game. Either way, you want to find a revenue stream and implement it. Not only will this help you earn enough money to keep the servers running, but investors will be impressed and might fund your company.

If you are having trouble figuring out how to monetize your platform, that's where the survey you have already done will come in handy. A simple question like this one will do the trick:

How much would you spend each month on upgrades in our game?

| a | $0 | b | $1 | c | $2.50 | d | $5 |
| e | $7.50 | f | $10 | | | | |

With data backing up your decisions, you have a much better chance in being one of the 18% of entrepreneurs who succeeds. Monetization goes hand in hand with user engagement. The more your users are engaged, the more likely they are to spend money on your platform.

User engagement is to startups as air is to humans. Without it, they can't survive.

Many startups have made their name (and fortunes) on user engagement rather than monetization. Instagram and Snapchat are two of those examples. There are many more. But don't count on that. Your goal should be to get both user engagement **and** revenue. It's like betting on a horse race where there are only two horses. If you have money down on both, you are sure to win.

Now that you understand a bit about how to turn your idea into a tangible product, here's a bit of homework for you. Learn how to use Twitter's Bootstrap framework to build a simple landing page where you can collect email addresses or pre-sell your product. Use Mailchimp or some other email service to store the emails so you can send out a newsletter later. Get at least 500 to 1000 beta testers to take your survey and enter their email address. Have them test the initial core value prop that you have built. You can do this by making an interactive mockup of your idea in a prototype builder like Invision. Or you can learn how to code the prototype by using Codecademy or Treehouse to add coding skills to your arsenal. Finding a CTO (Chief

Technical Officer) will be much easier later if you know how to code, even a little bit.

Or if you are creating a physical product, your homework is to pre-sell enough of your product to pay for the supplies you will need to build a prototype so that you can start a Kickstarter crowdfunding campaign.

Once you have iterated enough to the point where you are confident your idea will succeed in the market, it is time to build your Minimum Viable Product, or MVP. If you are a programmer or hardware engineer then you will be able to build it by yourself. If not, you will need to find a cofounder who can help you. So before we get into what an MVP is, let's talk about building your team.

Team Building

The first thing you must do before talking to people to whom you are potentially going to offer a position is have them sign an NDA (Non-Disclosure Agreement) before showing them any proprietary information, or letting them see your source code. Protecting your idea, IP (Intellectual Property), and your company is your first priority. If you've seen the movie, *"The Social Network,"* then you know what I'm talking about. If you haven't, then stop reading now, watch the movie, and then continue on. Without a signed NDA, someone could steal your idea and build it themselves. Although it's highly unlikely, it has happened. More often than not this won't be the case. This is because of the fact that ideas are just ideas, and the determining factor is not the idea, but rather the execution. Without the right people to properly execute the idea, it will never leave the whiteboard.

This is where choosing the right co-founder(s) and team members enters the equation. This process can be tricky and is mostly a balancing act. If you are well versed in business and marketing but don't have technical skills, then you'll be looking for a code ninja. If you know your way around Git and a command line, then you will need someone who knows how to make a killer PowerPoint presentation and can run your social media accounts like a boss. Most startups usually have two to three co-founders. Typically you will have your CEO (Chief Executive Officer), CTO (Chief Technical Officer), and CMO (Chief Marketing Officer) or VP of Marketing as that role is commonly known by.

In the beginning though, a title is just a title, and all co-founders wear many hats. Even if you are the lead developer, you still need to know a bit about business and marketing in order to make sure the technology fits the guidelines of your target market. This is especially crucial when it comes to UI & UX. When you choose your CTO, you need to make sure he or she understands the fundamentals of design for your particular market segment. If your market is aimed toward Millennials, then the UI/UX should reflect that demographic. For example, if the person you are vetting for the position was previously a developer for a financial analytics firm, they might not be the best fit since they mostly worked with enterprise software and numbers.

Alternatively, if the marketing guru you've been talking to worked for a meat company and knows their way around Twitter, they might not be the best fit for a vegan bakery who sells their baked goods through Facebook. I always say that you need to hire fast, and fire fast. You don't want to waste your time having several interviews with someone when you don't even know if they are capable of handling the work. So put them to work, and if they do great, they can continue; if not, let them go quickly.

Don't waste time waiting around for someone to eventually figure things out. You need bright individuals who don't need a ton of hand holding. So how do you make the right choices overall? Well, it's similar to how you vet your idea. You want to vet your co-founders and team members as well. This can be done in many ways.

The first (and my favorite) way is by testing them. What's great about testing people is that you can disguise it as work that you need done. A great example of this is the following. In one of my tech companies I needed a screen in my app to function a particular way. I asked developers to build a screen that would use the iPhone camera to record video in a certain aspect ratio, with a specific resolution, and with the interface I had designed. Then the video needed to be stored on the phone core data and be able to get uploaded to a profile in the app as well. Additionally, the video compression algorithm had to allow for ease of transfer without huge storage fees on my AWS (Amazon) server. The first person to get it right would get paid to do more work and earn performance based stock options as a member of our team.

We actually hadn't been able to figure it out on our own (at least not perfectly), so we "tested" a bunch of developers until one of them figured it out. That developer ended up being our lead developer for over a year and helped us build "Version two" of our app. So by making it seem like we were testing developers on their technical prowess, we were actually implementing a unique hiring strategy. This also works for marketing or any other department. You could easily put out a challenge to all marketing people that says, "The first person to get us 500 daily active users gets $500 and a potential salary, as well as company stock options." You can base it on a 90 day cycle of DAU analytics to make sure the users stick around and are engaging on your platform.

Another thing you can do to see what the potential hire is capable of is to have them write up a proposal stating what value they will add to your company. If they send you a document filled with amazing stuff, well then you know they are at least intelligent enough to touch on the right topics, and they might be the right fit for your company. If they don't send you anything at all, well then you didn't waste your time hiring and firing this person. Plus, what I love about the document assignment, is you can use what they wrote to fill in the Exhibit A for their Consultant Confidentiality and Inventions Assignment Agreement which you will need to have them sign before bringing them on board. Of course, you can add whatever other work you'd like them to perform as well, but at least you will have a good starting point as to where their skill set lies.

Lastly, the best way to truly find out what someone is made of, is to actually work with them. Typically I like a 30 day probationary period to see results. If after 30 days I'm not impressed, well then it's time to find someone else. But if after 30 days I am very happy with the results, then I would formally offer the person a position on my team. The first time you have to tell someone that you won't be bringing them on board is the closest thing you will have to firing someone, so it's good to get some practice before it actually happens.

I find that most tech entrepreneurs who haven't put in enough time or effort in building their startup by researching their market, gathering data, building a prototype, and learning the basics of programming fail to find willing co-founders or teammates. I've started companies where I had to pay programmers to build my prototype, and I've started companies where I learned how to code enough to build the prototype myself. Which one do you think succeeded?

I'm not saying you have to become a genius programmer. I'm saying that you should learn enough so that you at least understand how a database works, how the front end ties into it, the basics of UI / UX, the difference between coding languages such as JavaScript and PHP, or how APIs and frameworks can speed up the development process. When you have a thorough understanding of the technologies you want to implement, and are able to converse with your fellow developers about them, they will be more willing to work with you, especially if you built the prototype yourself. Then they will be flat out impressed and want to jump on board knowing they aren't the only developer on the team.

This goes for other departments as well. The more you learn about marketing, analytics, business, legal, finances, your market, and everything else, the easier it will be to find people for your team. Not only will you know what you're looking for, but you will know when they are good at what they do. I always try to do as much as I can by myself before seeking out team members. .

Do as much as you can by yourself until you need co-founders to get to the next level.

Once you have found your co-founders and other team members, whether they are interns, or management level employees, it's time to cover your bases with your legal documentation before everyone officially begins working.

Legal Documentation

This is a touchy subject for me, because my first tech startup was a complete failure due to the legal issues. Most entrepreneurs believe that as soon as they come up with an idea for a company, and they start talking to people about it, that they need to have a lawyer create documents for them to protect their company. Alternatively, there are resources like LegalZoom.com and RocketLawyer.com that provide those documents at a fraction of the cost of a lawyer. Of course, then you need to modify those agreements to fit your needs, which can be difficult to do if you do not understand legal jargon.

In the case of my first startup, although I understood technology, and had some basic marketing skills, I had a lot to learn. I partnered up with a friend of mine with whom I had worked on a film, and our interests were aligned to build a group-centric, social-commerce platform. There was nothing like it out in the market at the time (2009), so he was adamant about us obtaining legal counsel. Unfortunately, I was pressured into it, and he didn't give me a choice; it was either legal counsel, or no company. And since we had technically come up with the idea together, I felt as though I didn't have a choice.

So we visited a legal team my partner knew, and they went over all of the fees and services. After one year running the company, having monthly meetings with our legal counsel, getting contracts and agreements from them, and having them guide us through the legal process, we had spent roughly $7605. All of this was done without a prototype, a team, or really anything substantial. Yes, we had built a rudimentary website, landing page, social media accounts, and we did have somewhat of a "potential" team, but nothing was set in stone. Not only that, but the market started to creep up on us in our space, and we quickly got overtaken by companies that raised money.

Needless to say, my friend and I grew frustrated, and I was pretty upset in general. Since he had plenty of money at his disposal, the legal fees didn't really bother him that much. Many times, when he wanted to seek legal counsel, and I told him that we did not need to because we knew the answer, he still wanted to get the approval from our lawyers. He ended up paying more of the legal fees than I did, but I still had to pay at least $3000. At the time, I told him that I shouldn't have to pay that much because I didn't want to use the lawyers in the first place. Plus, I spoke up regarding the fact that I was doing all of the technology work (which was the bulk of the work).

I'll never forget what he said. "So you think that the work you are doing is worth more than the money I'm spending for our legal counsel?" Of course I answered, "Yes, I do. Big time!" Because without my work there would have been no company. I was the driving force behind everything. He literally laughed over the phone and said that I should just pay the legal bill. So I did. At that moment, I vowed to never put myself in a situation like that again.

The moral of the story is, do not seek legal counsel, or pay a lawyer anything, until you have at least a prototype, a solid team, and have the beginnings of a company forming with data proving that there is a place in the market for it. And even if you do have this, you do not need a lawyer in the beginning. You can easily use resources available online. With a little bit of hard work, research, and learning legal vocabulary, you should be able to modify existing online templates to suit your needs. As a matter of fact, I have a repository of documentation available on my website that will give you everything you need to get started. Of course, my documents are not the end all be all (and I'm not a lawyer), but they were created by lawyers and were very expensive. In my opinion, the most important legal documents are the ones that protect your IP.

When you begin talking to people who you might add to your team, you need to protect your IP before doing so. Actually, if you are doing it right, it's not your IP you are protecting, but your company's IP. Because when you form a new corporation, you'll want to assign your IP to the corporation. You might think, *"OMG, I won't own the IP anymore?"* That's correct, your company will own it. Why is that? Well, when an investor funds your company, they will want to make sure they are owning a piece of the IP. If you don't assign it over to the company, then you still own it, and your company doesn't own anything. Therefore the investor would be funding a company that doesn't own any IP. A smart investor wouldn't do that anyway, but with IP you have to make sure everything checks out.

The document used for the IP assignment is called an Intellectual Property Assignment and Confidentiality Agreement. This document does two things. First, it transfers ownership of the IP from you to the company. Secondly, it acts as an NDA as well. This document is usually reserved for the co-founders of the company. These co-founders typically own a hefty percentage of the company's Common Stock. The percentage of stock owned by co-founders depends on their roles in the company. For example, if you start a new S Corporation and you are the only founder and the CEO as well, then you own 100% of the company. If you add a CTO and co-founder to your company, you might offer them 50% of your company if they plan on doing half the work.

Here is another example: If you start the company with two co-founders, let's say a CTO and a CMO, maybe you'll offer your CTO 20% of the company, and your CMO 20% of the company. As CEO, you would then own the remaining 60% of the company. When you create the company, you will have to decide what type of company you want. The three main ones are an LLC (Limited Liability Company), a C Corporation, and an S Corporation. If you create an LLC, you will need to create an Operating Agreement (OA) that states the members' financial and managerial rights and duties. The percentages that the co-founders own would also be stated in the OA.

Now since an LLC is not a C or S Corporation, there is no common stock, so you would have to draft an additional document in your OA explaining that once you switch from an LLC to a C or S Corp the common stock will be issued from that company. It sounds confusing, but it's actually quite simple. Here's an easier way of putting it:

Dave has a metal detector and tells his friend Jen that if she helps him find gold coins on the beach he will give her 20% of the profits of whatever they find. He will keep the other 80% profit from the sale of the coins. To be fair, Dave gives Jen a written agreement that states these percentages, and they both sign it. They don't have a company yet, but in the agreement Dave writes that if they ever form a corporation, Jen will own 20% of the newly formed company.

So they go to the beach and find 10 gold coins. Dave sells the coins for $12,500. Dave keeps $10,000 (80%) and gives Jen $2,500 (20%). They buy another metal detector with some of the profits and go out the next day to find more coins. With both of them using a metal detector they find 80 gold coins, and sell the coins for $100,000. This time, instead of keeping the profits, they both agree to start a corporation and open a coin store. They form Dave & Jen's Treasures INC. as an S Corporation. Jen receives 20% common stock in the new corporation as per their signed agreement. Since the company has $100,000 in assets, she now owns $20,000 worth of the company **in stock**. Dave owns the other $80,000 **in stock**. The company owns the actual $100,000.

So now Dave and Jen want more help finding coins, so they use some of the money as a business expense to purchase more metal detectors and other equipment. They hire two more people and offer them 5% equity each in the company for a total of 10% equity. Those two new hires do not get common stock in the company because they are not co-founders. They receive non-qualified stock options that they will have the option to buy in the future. They also have to sign a Consultant Confidentiality and Inventions Assignment Agreement. Technically, Dave and Jen don't have to give them any stock, they could just pay them a salary instead. But they would rather save money this early in the company's growth, and therefore offer stock options instead. This way, if the two new hires do a good job, and the company grows, they benefit from dividends, salaries, or an acquisition later on.

Lastly, suppose a larger metal detector company comes in and wants to buy Dave & Jen's Treasures INC. for ten million dollars. Dave & Jen accept the offer and split the profit between themselves and the employees that have equity. Dave & Jen just became millionaires! The two employees earned $500,000 each after purchasing their 5% worth of stock options for pennies on the dollar.

Ok, now that I have given you a real life example, let me take a step back and explain a few things to you:

1. LLC vs. S corp vs. C corp
2. Common stock vs. Non-qualified stock options
3. Founder vs. Employee agreement
4. Operating agreement vs. Bylaws
5. Choosing your Board of Directors (BoD)
6. Choosing a percentage

First of all, instead of telling you the tax implications of each company type, I'll instead tell you the most common business use case. For example, if you are a graphic designer and want to start accepting work from companies on a contract basis, you could simply form an LLC and work for the company while paying yourself a salary. Forming an LLC absolves you of any liability and transfers it to the company. This way if you ever get sued, your personal assets are not at stake; only the company's assets are. An LLC is mostly used for what's called a lifestyle business, like a hairdresser, a fitness trainer, a bakery, or a business where you will earn a nice income to meet certain lifestyle requirements you seek. While you normally wouldn't take in an investor to scale your business, you might take a bank loan to grow a little.

Tech startups rarely form an LLC because LLCs aren't friendly to investors. Although laws have been changing to benefit entrepreneurs who form LLCs, a C corp is still more common in a tech startup. Investors favor C corps because they are taxable entities, they have a Board of Directors, and they use revenue to fuel growth. The downside is that C corps are taxed twice whereas S corps are not. But S corps don't offer the same benefits as a C corp, and therefore investors don't like them. A good rule of thumb is, if you are starting a business where you don't plan on raising VC (Venture Capital) money, then just form an LLC. If you plan on forming a company that will eventually give out common stock, stock options, and raise capital from outside investors, form a C corp. If you are still a bit fuzzy on this, there's a great thread on Quora that has a ton of comments[4].

Bottom line: Lifestyle business = LLC. The next Unicorn startup = C corp.

If you don't know what a Unicorn is, simply put, it's a company valued at $1 billion or more. If you're curious, I wrote an informative article that gives definitions to startup lingo[5]. So what's the difference between common stock and stock options? It's actually quite simple. Common stock is company equity held by co-founders and investors. This means that if you own common stock, you are an owner of the company. So if a company is worth $1 million, and you own 40% of the company, then your stock

---

[4]http://quora.jasonsherman.org
[5]http://lingo.jasonsherman.org

is valued at $400,000. This doesn't mean that you personally have $400,000 in the bank, it just means that is what your stock is valued at. Typically, co-founders get common stock because they are the ones who started the company.

On the other hand, if you have stock options, this means that you have the right, but not the obligation, to buy shares of the company for a fixed price during a certain time period. Usually, stock options are given to an employee on a performance basis, and they have the right to exercise the purchase of those options after a certain amount of time, say two to four years. For example, let's say you start a new company and build a mobile app. You have a CTO and a CMO as your co-founders, and all three of you hold common stock. Now that you have built your first app, and you take in funding from an investor, you want to hire a few more people to help scale your platform.

So you hire a developer, and a graphic designer. You would offer them performance based stock options after a thirty day grace period. Also, you would normally add a vesting period of two to four years into the stock option agreement. Vesting means they will earn the stock options each month. So for a two year period, that would be 24 months of vesting at 1/24th of their total amount per month. If you offer an employee 5% in stock options with a two year vesting period, that means they will earn a little more than 0.20% in stock options each month that they work with the company. If for any reason they quit working for the company before the vesting period is complete, they will have only earned the amount of stock options for the amount of time they worked. So let's say they only work for 12 months, well then they only earn 2.5% in stock options.

A good rule of thumb is that co-founders and investors receive common stock. Employees, consultants, interns, contractors and anyone else that you want to pay in equity will receive stock options. Now when I say "employees," everyone is an employee if they receive a salary. Even you, the CEO are an employee of the corporation, and you have a contract stating your salary. You can even be fired from your own company; just look at what happened to Steve Jobs at Apple. If you aren't the CEO, and instead are someone who is going to work for a startup, be careful when you first start working. Make sure that you have all contracts or agreements signed before starting to work with them. The last thing you want to do is give a startup your valuable time and skills only to be let go after a month, with nothing to show for it.

So why do founders and employees receive a different type of contract? Again, it's quite simple. Since founders own the company outright with their common stock, they don't have to earn it over time like employees do. Therefore their contract is in the form of the IP assignment, and the Operating Agreement, stating their roles and equity stakes. The exception is when a company gets funded by an investor. Usually the founders' shares go back to the company and vesting begins typically over a 2 to 4 year period. This way an investor makes sure the founders stay put and grow the company to profit or acquisition.

Employees sign a different contract. It's a combination NDA, IP assignment, as well as work description. It is typically called the Consultant Confidentiality and Inventions Assignment Agreement. You usually refer to "Exhibit A" in the agreement so that you can reference it when needed, and at the end of the agreement you can put the contents of Exhibit A for the consultant to read and accept as their job requirements. Here is an example work description for one of my developers:

EXHIBIT A

The following list is the work product description for the development consultant working on our mobile application. You will be in charge of and held responsible for the following:

1. Web Services implementation
2. API integration
3. UI/UX design and implementation
4. Database creation, modification, maintenance
5. Database scalability & security
6. Mobile (iPhone & Android) integration
7. Website version of application
8. Integrating frameworks
9. Version control on Github
10. Maintaining codebase on Github
11. Using best practices in code
12. Communicating with development team regularly
13. Database analytics and admin panel
14. Creating proper technical documentation
15. Providing KPIs (Key Performance Indicators) in easy to view charts

This is just one example of a work description I have given a developer for one of my startups. The reason you want to outline all of this in the agreement is that if for any reason they don't perform any of these tasks, you can terminate their contract immediately. This way, if they are upset and want to know why they are being terminated, you (and they) will have this contract to refer to. The termination conversation between you and a developer we will call Nicholas would go something like this:

You: I'm sorry Nicholas, but unfortunately your performance is not up to the standards we agreed to when we brought you on board.

Nicholas: Really? That sucks, I thought I was doing well…

You: Well yeah, you were doing well, but you weren't hitting point numbers 5, 9, 12, and 14. We needed you to perform those tasks and have brought it up to you before. We were hoping you would have changed your work habits and started doing them.

Nicholas: Man, I'm really sorry. I tried my best.

You: No problem. You earned six months' worth of stock options, and if you need a reference you can always put me down as one. Thanks again for working with us; we wish you the best of luck in your future endeavors.

If only they would go as smoothly as that! But you get the idea. By having this document, you are always protected, and the consultant will have no way of fighting the termination, because they agreed to the work description. This is exactly why it is vital that you get every consultant to sign an agreement. Most new entrepreneurs make the mistake of not signing any contracts or giving out agreements, and then everyone argues regarding what percentage they own, or who owns the IP. It can become a very sticky legal mess that you want to avoid at all costs.

While in an LLC the main document for structure is the Operating Agreement, in a C corp it is the Bylaws. A simple search on Google will tell you that the bylaws generally describe the functions of each corporate office, how shareholders' and directors' meetings are called and conducted, the formalities of shareholder voting, the qualifications of directors, the functions of board committees, and procedures for and limits on issuing and transferring shares. These provisions give structure on how the corporation is governed. You also have to keep Board Minutes during meetings that you have with your Board of Directors. Minutes are just another word for notes. You write them up after a meeting to record what took place during a board meeting. Maybe you hired new people and needed to get approval on equity you are going to give out. Or maybe you had to fire someone, or pivot your company to a new market. Either way, you will need to get board approval, and jot down board minutes to keep track of what took place.

You might be asking me, *'Well what is a board of directors, and how can I get one?'*

A BoD is a panel of experts in the field of industry in which your company exists. If you are building a new boat-sharing app, then most likely you will want an executive from Uber on your board of directors, or possibly even a boat racing champion. You need experts in the general ride-sharing space, the boat space, and maybe even an oceanographer. You never know what direction the company will go in, so you want to cover all your bases...or buoys in this case.

Now, you don't just get a BoD. You have to build a relationship with them, just as you do with your co-founders. A smart move is to work with an expert on an advisory level. This expert is basically a member of your Advisory Board, which is a more informal BoD. No paperwork is needed, and you can vet their skills. If you feel as though they bring value to your company, whether knowledge, connections, or funding, you can offer them a position (a board seat) on your BoD.

Keep in mind that once you form a BoD, you have to start treating your company differently. A number of things will happen. Here are a few of them:

- You have to host regular BoD meetings
- You have to write Board Minutes
- You have to hold a vote for important decisions
- Update your BoD on any company changes
- Hold meetings for hiring or firing of employees

Once you form a BoD, you can no longer make decisions on a whim. You have to get board approval. Think of it as having partners, and without your partner's approval, you can't move forward. If you start getting sloppy by making decisions on your own without getting board approval first, that's the kind of behavior that will get you kicked out of the CEO seat. A BoD is meant to help you, not hurt you, so use them wisely. Keep in mind that with certain decisions, they might not vote in your favor. They will usually have a good reason for voting against you. Hopefully you choose members for your board that share the same vision you do, so that when a vote does come up, they side with you.

Lastly, board members receive compensation for their involvement in your company. It's either a monthly cash stipend or company equity (common stock). When adding a member to your BoD, you both have to agree on the amount. They will have to sign a board approval to officially be added to your BoD. Then every time you want to add a new member, all members of the board have to sign the next approval. If the BoD doesn't vote a new member through, then you can't add them to your board.

Things can get tricky in a BoD when it comes to voting. Remember to choose your BoD wisely, because once they are in, it can be quite difficult to get them out.

Hopefully this chapter didn't bore you too much. If it did, I apologize. Unfortunately, this chapter could quite possibly mean the difference between success and failure, all because of a missing document.

As the old saying goes, *"It's always best to cross your t's and dot your i's."*

One of the questions asked most often by entrepreneurs looking to take on a co-founder is, "How much equity should I give them?" There are definitely industry standards, although not everyone adheres to them. Many variables come into play when disbursing equity to co-founders. Things such as:

- Skills, talents, value
- Time commitment
- Ideation involvement
- Domain expertise
- Connections to funding
- Previous successes
- Financial contributions

You can take any or all of these points into consideration when giving your co-founder equity. Let's say that you and a friend both came up with an idea at the same time. You did all of the business and marketing work, and your friend put in all the technology work. Well it might be safe to say that you have both earned 50% of the company. Then again, maybe you are a programmer, and you built a mobile app all by yourself. You launched it on the app stores and are already earning a bit of revenue from the app. Your friend says he/she loves the idea and wants to help you further market the app. So you look at your friend's prior experience, knowledge, and what value they add to your team. You might decide to give your friend 10% of the company based on these factors. There's a fantastic equity calculator on Foundrs.com that you can try out[6].

Ultimately, you have to ask yourself, what would happen if your co-founder walked away from the company. Would you be screwed? If the answer is yes, then they are valuable to your company, and instrumental to your success. Therefore they might deserve a larger equity stake, say 20-50%. If the answer is no, then maybe you can get away with giving them 2-5%. In the end, if they agree to the equity you offer, then there is no harm done.

Let's say that you just graduated from college with a degree in International Business, and you don't know the difference between HTML and LOL. You have an idea for a new mobile app that tells you what breed of dog is seen through your camera. Sounds like you are in dire need of a

---

[6]http://foundrs.com

CTO. You meet with a friend who you know is really good at building websites and mobile apps. He likes the idea, and says he can build the iPhone and Android apps, database, and website. Now you have to decide on how much equity to give him as a co-founder.

Here's a good question for you. How much would you have to pay someone in cash to do all that? $5,000? $20,000? $50,000? $100,000? The answer depends on several factors. Each person has a different view on money, time, and value. A college student who is a killer developer might think $5,000 is a lot of money. How much pizza and coffee can they buy with $5,000? A lot! Then again, a 35 year old married father of two kids, with a mortgage, two cars, school loans, and a ton of other bills will need a lot more than that, probably $50,000 or more. While the college kid with barely any bills might take 5% equity, the 35 year old will probably want 20%. Again, you have to decide on the equity based on variables, and the co-founder has to agree to the equity.

For example, in the past I was given 12% equity in one company as a CTO, 45% equity in another company as COO, and have owned over 50-80% equity in startups that I founded with other co-founders. Percentages will vary from company to company; just make sure that you are happy with the percentage you get. Once you put your percentages in your CAP table (Capitalization Table), they are pretty much set in stone, especially if your BoD approves them.

Your CAP table provides an analysis of the founders' and investors' percentage of ownership, equity dilution, and value of equity in each round of investment. This is typically a spreadsheet, and contains formulas that help you determine dilution every time you give out shares either to founders, employees, or investors. Dilution is when everyone's shares are affected by equity being given out. Simply put, it means when you give out equity, your equity, and everyone else's equity is cut down to compensate for the equity given out. It has to come from somewhere, right?

Besides equity, there is also the potential for a salary around the corner, if and when you get funding for your company. Equity is not the only thing you will get when you own part of a company. Salary is determined the same way as equity, although in the beginning, most founders earn the same amount, say $50,000 each until there is more money to throw around. I hear stories of founders paying themselves $100,000 a year each (I'm not going to name any names), and then they run out of money and their startup crashes and burns. Well, duh. Idiots.

In my opinion, it's common sense to spend as little money as possible in the beginning of a new startup. This book is called "Strap on your Boots," not "Strap on your Gucci's." The point of bootstrapping is to do as much work as you can by yourself, without paying outside development shops, graphic designers, marketing companies, PR firms, lawyers, accountants, and any other contractors. Do as much as you can by yourself while spending as little money as possible. You want people on your team that can do the same thing.

Overall, when you are building a team you have to make sure that your documents are prepared and correct. Cover your bases with contracts, equity disbursement, co-founder vetting, your advisory board, and everything else I listed in this chapter (and even some things that I missed or left out!).

A startup is kind of like a race car driver. The driver needs an owner, manager, sponsors, engineers, mechanics, crew chief, pit crew, and a team of other people. The driver can't win a race without all of these people on his team. Similarly, your idea alone doesn't stand a chance, but the right team backing you up might just get you to the finish line!

Minimum Viable Product

If you made it this far, that means you vetted your idea, put together a kickass team, have your documentation taken care of, and are ready to build the next big thing. Now it's time to build your Minimum Viable Product, or MVP. What exactly is an MVP? Simply put, it is the most barebones minimum version of your product that you can build to generate enough interest from the market and/or investors. Besides raising money, building your MVP will be the most challenging part of your journey to success.

The first thing you have to think about when building your MVP is what you want it to include. I can almost guarantee you, whatever it is that you want to include, it will be too much. Every time I sit down with an entrepreneur and they pitch me their idea or their MVP, it is usually a full scale platform, not an MVP. This goes back to your core value prop and how you implement it in your MVP.

For example, let's say your idea is to build a mobile app that helps college students buy and sell their used stuff on campus to earn some extra cash. Here's what you probably think your MVP should include:

1. Signup / login screen linked to your college email
2. Profile screen for personal info
3. Search screen with filters such as:
   a. Price range
   b. Item category
   c. Item condition
   d. Location
   e. Seller reputation
4. Communication system (instant chat or emailing) for buyer & seller
5. Camera integration to take pictures of items you want to sell
6. Item listing screen
7. Payment processing for purchases
8. Fraud detection and protection
9. Shipping system if in a different state
10. Rating and review system
11. Social media sharing integration

I'm sure you can add plenty of other items to this list. But for now this list will get you a solid first version, right? Not really. This is what I would call a full blown Version 2.0, with all the features you would need in order to scale to a unicorn size company. Actually, it sounds a lot like eBay, right?

Initially your idea was to help students earn some extra cash by selling their stuff. In order to break down the process of figuring out what to include in your MVP, you have to decide on the most crucial features or functions that are needed in order for you to get a college student to make his or her first sale on your app. The best way to do this is by using what's called lean methodology. Believe it or not, everything you have read up until this point is partly based on the principles of lean methodology. So what is it?

Lean methodology is getting the most value for your customer while spending as little time or resources in the process.

I'm pretty sure I've shown you how to do that so far. An extra step you can take to make sure you have all your ducks in a row, is to create a lean canvas. This helps you truly define each part of your company in a visual way, so that everyone in your startup is on the same page. You can do this at LeanStack.com; here is what my lean canvas looks like for Instamour:

Instamour - Lean Canvas

PROBLEM

For singles dating wastes time and money. Emailing, picture/text profiles don't solve this.

Picture & Text Profiles

Emailing is broken

Wasted time & money

EXISTING ALTERNATIVES

Skype

WhatsApp

Facebook

Google Hangouts

Meeting in person

Exchanging phone #s

SOLUTION

Instamour gives you an accurate impression of your prospective date through live and recorded video and chat.

Video profiles

video, phone or instant chat

Meet on the app first

KEY METRICS

user base

amours made

api calls

video calls

phone calls

instant chats

comments made

UNIQUE VALUE PROPOSITION

Save time and money by mitigating risk through video

HIGH-LEVEL CONCEPT

Instamour = Skype for Dating

CUSTOMER SEGMENTS

25-45 singles

Single College Students

Single Professionals

Single Mothers

Single Fathers

EARLY ADOPTERS

Dating app users

Video app users

Messaging app users

UNFAIR ADVANTAGE

Video compression algorithms.

Merging of videos

Unique communication area.

Live on cross platform

CHANNELS

Social media

Press

Events

newsletter

blogging

video production

COST STRUCTURE

Recurring Costs: Rent, Salaries, Travel, Hosting

Brand Ambassador:

Marketing - Trade Shows, Swag. Event hosting/sponsorships

User Acquisition Programs

- Direct install (Outsourced UA companies PPA)

- Preinstalled on phone when delivered after purchase

REVENUE STREAMS

Google AdSense

In app purchases (Includes gifting to other members)

In app upgrades

Video Ads

Monthly Subscriptions

Lean Canvas is adapted from The Business Model Canvas (BusinessModelGeneration.com) and is licensed under the Creative Commons Attribution-Share Alike 3.0 Un-ported License

So let's continue. Clear your mind of anything regarding technology, smartphones, computers, social media, and the Internet in general. Imagine you live in a time where none of that exists. How would you get your first sale then? Well, personally I would post flyers on a college campus, or simply set up a table in the quad to see if anyone has any stuff they want to sell. College students always want to make extra money, and they usually have stuff to sell such as: video game consoles, old phones, clothes, used books, etc.

Once I get a few bites and students drop off their things to me in order to sell them, I would find the buyers. I can do the same thing again, post flyers with the items for sale and their prices, or just set the items up on a table for sale in the quad. This is the easiest and most likely oldest way of buying and selling items. Once I sell the items, I would then give 70% of the profit to the sellers and keep 30% for performing the transactions. Word might spread that students are earning cash through me and I might just have a new business opportunity on my hands. On the other hand, if for some reason I can't get any items from students or subsequently can't get anyone to buy the items, then I can stop right there. I vetted the business, it didn't work, and so I didn't waste much time or resources. That's lean methodology. Now apply it to the app idea.

Remember the list I wrote that explained what you think the app might need? I'll give you a minute to go back and look at it again. If you want to get your first cash sale by using lean methodologies, this is what the list should actually look like:

1. Method of listing an item for sale
2. Method of buyer contacting seller

That's it. Nothing else. You need to list an item for sale, and you need someone to buy that item. If you can do that just once and earn even just one dollar, you can probably do it again. Do it 100 times while earning a commission on each sale, and you have a business. Then, and only then, can you start working on the original list, minus some items. Some of you might be wondering how you can accomplish even just the two items I listed above. I'm going to teach you a powerful word: Leverage.

Leverage existing technologies, whether open source, SDKs, APIs, or otherwise to achieve your goal without building a thing.

Leveraging technology is something that I have done for practically every company I have founded. Why build a video hosting site, when you can use YouTube's API (Application Program Interface)? Or in the case of this buying & selling app, why build your first MVP when you can leverage something like WPauctions.com? For $39 you can buy their eCommerce system that works on any device. That's a small price to pay to test your theory. By leveraging this existing technology, you can white label it and give it your college campus colors, your own logo, etc. By having students use this, you are reaping all the rewards, while not having built a thing! Of course you have to do some research, learn a little Wordpress, and set up the software in the first place. But you can probably do all that in a few days. That's a lot better than several months (or years), right?

Remember, the first question you want to ask yourself before building your first MVP is, *"Can I leverage existing technology to test my theory?"* More often than not you will find that there is an existing solution out there waiting for you to use. Once you have tested your theory, gathered data, and are happy with the results, then you can move forward. Don't forget, the list I wrote out was a full blown Version 2.0; so how do you determine what is a good Version 1.0? Well that is just a tad more complicated, and the answer comes with experience. There is definitely a rule of thumb or two when it comes to deciding on the features of your first version.

You have your initial idea of listing an item for sale and a buyer contacting a seller. Now you want to expand those a bit in order to build an actual platform. WPauctions is a great start, but you can't really scale that, and you don't technically own the IP. What you need to do is take your initial list and separate it into two categories: Need & Want. Here's how mine would look:

NEED

1. Signup / login screen / college email

2. Profile screen for personal info

3. Item listing screen

4. Search for categories

5. Emailing for buyer & seller

6. Social media sharing integration

WANT

1. Search screen with filters such as:
   a. Price range
   b. Item category
   c. Item condition
   d. Location
   e. Seller reputation

2. Instant chat for buyer & seller

3. Camera integration to take pictures

4. Payment processing for purchases

5. Fraud detection and protection

6. Shipping system if in a different state

7. Rating and review system

Everything on the "Need" side would be considered your MVP or Version 1.0 - and everything on the "Want" side is your Version 2.0, if and when your MVP is a success. There are actually a couple of other reasons why it's smart to separate your versions. It has to do with the Apple iTunes store and the Google Play store, if you are building a mobile app. The app stores give special treatment and even feature apps who are updated more often than others. They realize that you, the developer are working hard on fixing bugs, and enhancing the user experience for your users. This gets people to come to the app stores more often, which might result in a purchase.

Unlike SEO (Search Engine Optimization), app store search works much differently. Instead of having to search through millions of webpages, you have to search through millions of apps. The only way to get higher up on the list is by submitting updates to your app regularly, once every two weeks for example, and having a lot of people download your app of course. Of course, getting mentioned in the news causes a big uptick in downloads, but that growth rarely stays consistent. So by leaving a lot of features out of your app, you can add one every two weeks to your platform, submit an update, and make the app stores happy knowing that you are constantly improving your app.

If you have a smartphone, then you have probably noticed your apps updating pretty regularly. Do you ever read the list of things that they improved in the app? Sometime it's just a bug fix and sometimes a new feature.

Other times it's a complete rehaul of the interface. Doesn't that usually make you click on the app to open it and see what the improvement was? Bingo, that's the second reason this is smart to do: user engagement. App companies know that by submitting regular updates, users are more prone to click on the app to find out what was upgraded or fixed. So the user engagement goes up and your user's app search ranking goes up, so you get two for the price of one.

The last reason is similar to the second, but it's more about a subconscious method of reaching your users. By submitting regular app updates, your users feel that you are working around the clock to make the app better, which in turn makes them appreciate the app more. Plus, if you launch a new feature and your users really like it, they will spread the word on social media and tell their friends. So think of your versions more in terms of app updates (if they are mobile), and increasing app store ranking, user engagement and user feelings. If you are only building a website, it works differently. You still want to keep your MVP simple, but you are able to submit updates whenever you want and it doesn't really affect the search results. Plus, with a website you don't have to wait for app store approvals, which can take weeks in some cases for Apple iTunes.

So now you have your MVP list of what you need to build in order to properly execute a Beta (your first semi-public) launch. Since you have a decent amount of email addresses already from your previous tasks, you should have a good pool of users to help you test your Beta platform. Since you have put together a great team, I am assuming you now have a technical co-founder, or a couple of developers on your team who can build your MVP. Maybe you are the programmer and you are going to build it yourself. Either way, now is the time for you to choose the technology stack you will build your platform on. A tech stack is a combination of software products and programming languages used to create a web or mobile application. Applications have two software components: client-side and server-side, also known as front-end and back-end.

Explaining to you how to choose the right tech stack could be a book in and of itself. So I'll keep this short and simple. The first thing you have to figure out is what will be the end device used for your platform. What I mean is, do you want people to use your platform on a computer (whether desktop or laptop), or do you want people to download an app to their mobile phones? Keep in mind, even if you build this for the web, you can build a responsive website that conforms to mobile devices. Personally, I love using Twitter's framework called Bootstrap[7]. It's free, pretty easy to learn, and you can build an endless amount of UIs (User Interfaces) with it. A framework is another word for a library. It is an underlying structure that allows you to build things quicker by using code snippets and pre-built functions that speed up the

---

[7]GetBootstrap.com

development process. Remember how I said to leverage open source technology? Bootstrap is one of them.

Now, if you are building for the web, in my opinion the best way to go initially would be to build a JavaScript platform, both front and backend. This means using something like ReactJS with a NodeJS backend database. You can always build the frontend in JavaScript and the backend in PHP / MySQL, or even Ruby on Rails for the whole thing. Ultimately, you have to decide which tech stack you feel most comfortable with, which you can learn, or which languages your CTO already knows.

For example, if you are building a video platform with social aspects, you may want to work with JavaScript or Ruby on Rails. On the other hand, if you are building an enterprise analytics SaaS (Software as a Service) platform, you may want to stick with .Net, C#, or Java. E-commerce sites typically use PHP / MySQL, but you don't have to go with PHP. You can build it with whatever you want. Just make sure that whatever technology you choose, your team is an expert in those languages. Also, make sure you feel comfortable enough with your chosen tech stack that if you have to bring somebody new on board, that they will be able to jump right into the code base as well.

Once, my team and I built a platform in Java, and when the developers hit many walls we had to find someone to try and fix the issues. The problem was, we couldn't find a Java developer who was good enough to do that. So we ended up rebuilding the whole thing in

JavaScript (ReactJS & NodeJS) and got the end result we were looking for. So choose wisely when you are going to build your MVP; you don't want to lose valuable time and resources by picking the wrong language.

When it comes to mobile apps, realistically you really only have two choices. The first is using a cross platform technology such as PhoneGap.com. The second is building the apps natively in Apple's Xcode (or Swift), or Google's Android Studio. If you use a cross platform technology, you will be able to build your application once, and then wrap it in different packages for iPhone, Android, Windows phone, etc. The downside is that typically the apps will not perform as well as they will natively. I find that there is a bit of a lag on those apps; the functionality isn't always there, and certain features are more difficult to integrate.

If you build your app using a native technology, you are using the actual code that was meant to be displayed and used on the devices, and therefore you get a much more fluid experience both tactilely, and functionality wise. All the apps I've ever built have always been native. I have never used a cross platform technology, although I am not opposed to it, I just feel as though the native experience is much smoother.

Assuming you have a CTO, you should have a handle on what languages you want to use, what (if any) frameworks you will build off of, where you will host your platform, what type of database you want to build, and how you want it all to fit together. Before you actually build anything, you want to create what is called a workflow document along with workflow maps. I do this for every new startup that I create.

Here is the workflow document for the app I mentioned earlier that I came up with 4 years ago and which Godaddy recently launched:

1) **Sign up / Sign in Screen**
   a) Sign in button
   b) Sign up button
   c) Demo the app button - if you push it, you can browse the app but you cannot post anything or interact with users..
2) **Login**
   a) Sign in with LinkedIn button
   b) Sign in with Facebook button
   c) Sign in with Gmail button
   d) Sign in with Email address & Password
   e) Forgot Password Button
3) **Authentication – LinkedIn sign up**
   a) Sign in w/ LinkedIn uses LinkedIn email & password to pull your name, photo, profile overview, college degree, connections, contact info, company pages, location, etc.
   b) Also for your profile to be complete you can add your skills & expertise, achievements, certifications and you can choose categories of interest as well to show in your feed.
4) **Authentication – Facebook, Gmail sign up**

a) Sign in w/ Facebook automatically uses Facebook email & password as well as full name and profile photo.
b) A user who signs up with Facebook must fill in the rest of their profile on their own.
c) This is the same for Gmail.

5) **Authentication - Email sign up**
   a) choose profile photo (Camera or Gallery option)
   b) Full name
   c) email address (check to see if email already exists)
   d) password - can't be blank, no minimum characters, can be anything
   e) A user who signs up with email must fill in the rest of their profile on their own.

6) **Preview the app**
   a) User will be directed to the feed where they can see ideas.
   b) A message appears when a user clicks on the left nav or custom search, or any of the icons such as vote up, comment, collaborate, or share that says, "To interact with our members you need to Sign in or Create an account." By pressing "OK", the user will be directed to sign in / sign up screen. By pressing "Cancel", they can continue checking out ideas.
   c) Most recent ideas appear at the top of the feed.

7) **Nav Menu**
   a) Home: takes a user to the main feed
   b) My Ideas: takes a user to the ideas they posted to edit, delete, share, etc.
   c) Messages: takes a user to see their messages from other members. They may read, respond, or delete messages here.

d) My Groups: takes a user to manage and interact with their groups.

e) Notifications: takes a user to the notification screen so they can see the various notifications.

f) Share: opens a screen to share using Facebook, Twitter, LinkedIn, Google+, Email, SMS.

g) Profile: takes a user to their profile so they may add things or edit their profile.

h) Settings: takes a user to their settings to change things like push notifications, email, password, and other settings.

8) Post an idea

a) User has 141 characters to type out their idea

b) They may click the # sign at the bottom right of the keyboard (must be present in code) while typing the idea and the # sign will appear in light red text in the message field. User can type a keyword after the #, and when they click space, the #keyword will be in light red.

c) User must choose a category (middle left icon) to put their idea in.

d) Optional: user can add their location (middle middle icon).

e) Optional: user can add a photo or drawing (middle right icon).

f) When finished, user clicks "Post" and the idea will be posted in the respective category with all options included and keywords showing up like so: #keyword in the post.

9) Feed interaction

a) Idea feed shows most recent ideas along with the photo and name of the user who posted it.

b) Each idea has 4 icons below as well as the category listed next to the icons.

c) Light bulb icon is for "likes" or "vote up". The more it has, the higher the idea goes in the feed.

d) Comment icon is for people to leave comments.

e) Collaborate icon is for people who would like to collaborate. If they click it, they can add a short message as well as add skills (from the database) to the message for the idea creator to review. If the idea creator accepts the collaborator into their group, a notification will be sent to the collaborator. The idea creator may close the idea & the group once they have reached the desired number of collaborators. At this point, the idea will not be on the feed anymore but will become the topic of a new group for the collaborators.

f) Share icon is to share the idea via SMS, email, or Facebook, Twitter to get others involved.

g) Category link is a shortcut to see more from that category.

10) **Search Box**

a) You can search using a keyword to see all ideas from that keyword. Top ten keywords are available to click on if you would like a shortcut.

b) You can also search by choosing one of our preset categories to see all ideas from that category.

c) You may also choose a distance if you would like to see ideas in your area to make it easier to collaborate.

d) Once you click "Search" the ideas will populate on the feed from most recent to least recent.

11) **Settings - Account**

a) Email Address - lets you change your email address

b) Change Password - lets you change your password
c) Update Location - uses GPS to change location
d) Push Notifications – on or off
e) Alerts - Where you can see public or private messages such as: telling you to input more info for your profile, or add a photo, or you have a new collaborator message waiting, etc. - and we can have the numbered notification in the settings tab as well as the Account tab for alerts. These will show up as push notifications.

12) Push Notifications
a) An idea got voted up
b) An idea got a comment
c) I received a collaborator request
d) Someone shared my idea
e) New message received

13) Support
a) Rate our app - Takes you to Grabea on the app store
b) Send us feedback - Opens up an email premade to send to us with the subject line saying, "I have an idea for Team Grabea!"
c) Delete account - Confirming message
d) About Grabea - About screen (from the web)
e) Privacy policy - Privacy screen (from the web)
f) Terms of service - Terms screen (from the web)

14) Logout
a) Log out. Sends you to Login screen

15) Notifications
a) app icon should have badge with the total count of pending notifications or alerts
b) Brain icon in navbar should have a number showing how many notifications there are, same goes for the

nav menu when you click on the brain, it will show notification #, messages #, group #, etc.

c) web server should send push notifications about new notifications

d) Push Notifications should have a custom sound created by Grabea. Same goes for messages, we should have our own sounds.

16) Special Notes

a) I want most images that are not icons (buttons) to be either just text, or RGB color behind text. For example, for "Sign up" & "Sign in" buttons, those should not be buttons. Those should be color behind text. The less images the app has, the smaller the file size will be, and the faster it will load. Same goes for the navigation menu. I want it to be text & icons over RGB.

b) When screens are loading, I want a thin loading bar in the navbar showing.

As you can see, it is very detailed and tells the CTO exactly what I envision the app to do. In addition to the workflow document, you can create a visual workflow map or wireframe to show what the workflow document looks like. Using a whiteboard is fine for this process. You can see my whiteboard, flowchart, and app design on the article that I posted earlier in the Ideation chapter.

By creating this document and wireframe, it allows you and your team to go over every aspect of your platform to make sure that everyone understands what every single button, menu, feature or function does. This way, if there are any underlying questions or issues, you can address them before wasting valuable time and resources building something and then having to fix it later. Also, if for any reason you need to outsource your project to a developer in another country, then you definitely need these documents so that everything is crystal clear. Nine out of ten times, people aren't happy with the results from outsourcing because *they didn't get what they wanted.* Well then, make sure you tell them exactly what you want with a detailed workflow document and wireframes, maps, mockups, etc.

Another way to put together your workflow document (and I've said this before), is to research your space thoroughly. Again, I like to use Flipboard and Product Hunt, but there's also a really cool website called Pttrns.com that shows you designs of apps. You can see every single screen from a multitude of apps to get a feel for what's out there. Then, I recommend that you download and sign up for as many platforms in your space as possible, and use them as much as you can. These are some of the features that I would want you to look at and study:

- The login process
- The profile creation process
- How do you upload a video
- How to post a comment
- How to become friends with someone
- How to choose an item to purchase (shopping cart)
- The purchasing system
- Dashboard and analytics

- The main home screen
- Icons, text, colors, menus
- Any camera features
- How many steps things take
- Account settings

There are plenty of other features and functions you can test, but this list should give you a good starting point. By using and testing various apps, you will get a feel for the UI/UX in your space. This will help you make better decisions when you are creating a document and creating your design. I'm not saying that you should copy these platforms, but I am definitely saying that they should inspire you. Maybe you will find things that you don't like from these apps that you can fix. Don't forget, a lot of new platforms are just better versions of other platforms. Again, remember Myspace vs Facebook? Always research and rigorously test the UI/UX in platforms that lie within your space.

If you are building a hardware product, then buy your competitors' products and test them. What don't you like about them? What could you make better? Is the material cheap? Do the features and functionality work specifically for what you are looking for in the product? If you can 3D print a prototype of your product and show it to people who would use your product, you'll be able to find out what they like and don't like about it. Having a physical product to show people will be much better than showing them a picture of it. If you don't have a physical product to show off, you can always go to stores and see people use certain products. How do they hold it in their hands? How do they wear it? How do they put it in their pocket? You want to discover every single aspect of products in your space and the behavior people emit when using them.

Now that you have determined exactly what it is you want to build, you still need to keep in mind that you will be adding more features onto your platform down the road. When you build your database and your platform, make sure you build it in a modular way, where you will be able to add new modules onto your existing framework. Also, a good rule of thumb when building a platform is to include an API (Application Program Interface), so that you can tie into various technologies, and allow other developers to tie into it much easier. An API is a set of routines, protocols, and tools for building software applications. An API specifies how software components should interact and APIs are used when programming graphical user interface (GUI) components.[8] When you sign up for a new website using your Facebook login, the website is using Facebook's API to facilitate the profile creation process. This way the website gets your picture, name, email, password, location, employment history, and any other piece of information the website needs to create your profile. This is just one way to leverage an API.

---

[8] http://api.jasonsherman.org

I can't tell you how many times entrepreneurs come to me with a platform asking me for help, and I find out that they built an extremely large platform, with a million features, no API or documentation, and they don't even know how to manage the code. First of all, you need to be storing your code in a repository such as Github.com. This also helps you collaborate with other developers. Secondly, you need to document everything, so that if another developer joins your team, they can read your documentation, and jump right into the code without having to spend a ton of time learning how you built it.

Just because you are building an MVP, that doesn't mean you shouldn't be thinking about your next version. As a matter of fact, you should be. Because if your MVP is successful, and you are actually able to raise funding, investors will want to know what you're going to do with their cash. By having a plan to implement new features already laid out, they will be not only impressed, but will feel confident that you are going to succeed even further. Part of building your platform this way also means you need to take scalability into account. How many users can access your platform at the same time, and use certain features at the same time, without crashing your server? That's one example of scalability.

Another would be if you own a mobile dog grooming business. You have a van and are able to groom twenty dogs a week by driving around to people's houses. The question is, how can you scale this to 100 vans, and

2000 dogs a week? Maybe you can't. That's something you need to think about also. Is my idea scalable? If not, it may just be a lifestyle business, which I mentioned earlier in the book. Investors like scalability. Take Uber for example. They started with a handful of cars and just gave people rides locally until they started to turn a profit. Then they scaled to almost 200,000 drivers and over one billion rides a day in just a few years.

One of the biggest keys to success is building a platform to perform with simplicity in mind. The only features you should include are the ones that will get you the crucial data that will help you make the decisions on what to build next.

I always tell entrepreneurs the age old saying: "Keep it Simple Stupid" (K.I.S.S.).

It really does work, especially in this day and age when Millennials' attention spans are so much lower than they used to be. To keep up with this ever changing attention span, you have to make things simple, fast, fun, engaging, and useful. The more you complicate your platform, the more features you add, and the more steps each feature needs, the less successful your platform will be. Don't forget, you can always complicate things later and add a ton more features, once you have a loyal user base. Look at how Facebook started from just a newsfeed and the ability to post a status update, to now being able to create user groups, event pages, upload photo albums, play games with friends, and so many other features. Rome wasn't built in a day, and your vision for a complete platform won't be either. Be patient, keep things simple, and you will succeed.

Using the same methodologies I outlined earlier in the book, once you build your MVP, you should be testing it with your beta pool of users, gathering data from analytics and from surveys, iterating your software based on the data that you received, tweaking your platform, and then repeating the process until you get the results that you are ultimately looking for. This is key in your tech startup early on. This is also the biggest reason large companies can't copy your idea as quickly as you can iterate.

Let's say you create a new website that helps people figure out their sugar content to monitor their diabetes. Your idea is unique because you created a USB device where you can insert a drop of your blood. Through this device and your software, users will receive amazing health data that they had to previously get from a doctor's visit. Based on data, after a few months you have determined that you have a great idea, and so you release it to the public after your MVP is successful. Then a few months later, you notice that a large pharmaceutical company comes out with something similar. But what they didn't know was that this whole time that they were copying you, you were iterating on your original idea. Your tweaked device now gives you results for a lot of other things and not just diabetes.

Which device is better? The one that monitors your diabetes? Or the one that monitors your diabetes, weight, blood pressure, liver, and overall health statistics? The point is, you shouldn't worry about companies copying your idea, because more than likely they will have to go through the bureaucracy of management, ownership, and then spend time and resources on putting together a team to build this product or platform. Whereas your nimble startup is able to iterate quickly based on data and tweak your platform quickly. Think of your size as your advantage over larger companies. You may have heard Kevin O'Leary say on Shark Tank, *"What makes you so special? Why can't I just hire a few people to build this and crush you like the cockroaches you are?"* Well that's just it, you are small, nimble, and able to react quickly to the market. Plus you have spent the better part of six months gathering data, researching your market, building your user base, and making decisions based on all the data. You have a much better chance at success than a large company does. And for whatever reason, you notice the market is getting too saturated, or a competitor is taking your market share; well then you can do what many startups before you have done: Pivot.

A great example of pivoting and how it can mean the difference between failure and success is that of a company called Tote that came on the eCommerce scene in 2009. Tote gave users a way to window shop on their phones and put together a list of items they wanted to purchase in the future. One of their main issues back in 2009 was that payment processing had a very low friction rate. But the users on Totes platform were each amassing a big list of items and so the founders decided to pivot, based on their users' behavior. In 2010 Tote pivoted to Pinterest, and now they are worth billions of dollars.

I have personally pivoted a startup twice, and am in the middle of building a vertical of my most successful startup. A vertical is different from pivoting because instead of just closing up shop and changing your idea completely to something else, you find a niche in your market that is very similar to the one you are already in. Let's say you build a skyscraper, and you want to build another one. You wouldn't knock down the first one to build the second one. You would just build the skyscraper next to the first one. You might build the skyscraper using the same building materials, but both buildings might have a different use. One might be an office building, and the other an apartment building. Two buildings with the same foundation and materials, but with different uses.

With my video dating app Instamour, investors kept telling me that they would rather invest in a B2B, revenue driven, SaaS. After hearing that a couple of hundred times, I decided to act on their suggestion. See2B was born to help businesses communicate with their customers via their website through custom code without having to leave the site to use another video chat tool. This eliminates the friction of email addresses, usernames, phone numbers, installation of programs, plugins, etc.

Essentially, pivoting will happen at the moment where you believe you need to shut down your company because you have no other choice. That's when you can see if there is something you can change about your business, or leverage your technology and your team, to simply go in a different direction. Many startups have done this in the past and have succeeded.

One of the hardest things that you will ever have to do with your startup is decide whether you can pivot, or if you have to actually close down the company. Although it is a very difficult decision that you will have to make at some point, it is one that you should make quickly. You never want to waste time trying to keep a company alive that is destined to fail. There are many famous sayings out there about this, and one of the most prevalent that I've heard is, *"Fail fast. Fail often."*

It means that if you feel as though you are in the midst of failing, and you can't pivot, don't waste another minute. Close down the company, take a break, and start something else. If it happens again, close the company down quickly. Failing often means that maybe you have learned enough lessons and have become an expert to the point that potentially your third startup will finally succeed. If you can fail fast and often, eventually you should be able to succeed in one of your ideas quickly. As an example, one of my cofounders and I had to close down See2B about a year after starting it. We posted a blog about it and sent it off to the Philly tech community as well as social networks. Many entrepreneurs praised us for our efforts, mainly because we used our methodologies to solidify each aspect of our MVP. Unfortunately, Philly is a tough market when it comes to early-stage (seed) funding.

Even though we did everything the right way, we still couldn't build quite enough to further prove out our beta. Even with all the hard work you and your cofounders put in, you will still always need a really good development team. In this market where the demand for good programmers is high, the supply is very low. If you are reading this book, I would implore you to learn to code. Even if it's only good enough to build a functional responsive website for your company. One of the biggest issues that always takes place with tech startups is that they need programmers to build their idea in order to get funding. If you become a programmer, then you are removing that wall. I'm not saying you have to be the most incredible developer around, but if you can build a prototype you are good to go. There are tons of open source software, frameworks, and video tutorials on various websites like I mentioned earlier. Attracting talent is much easier when you are talented yourself.

One advantage to building a platform in a certain space (in this case video) is when you build another platform in the same space it will take you much less time, and you'll be able to avoid a ton of mistakes. For example, another startup I'm the COO and product manager for is in the video space. It's called InVidMe, and it's a fun, interactive video entertainment platform. We faced similar challenges building the video compression algorithms and camera UI as I did previously in Instamour. So by knowing the blockages we would most likely face, I was able to help my development team navigate the coding process with ease. Not only were we able to quickly overcome any wall that we hit, but we were able to launch the MVP within a handful of months. It's quite incredible if you think about it. Especially with the fact that we basically had to invent a whole new camera system and video process.

During the MVP stage of your startup, one of the most important things you have to come up with in order to attract talent, users, mentors, and even potential investors is your name and branding. Choosing a name, designing a logo, and coming up with your brand takes a lot of research and time. There are various tools I use to expedite this process. To choose my domain names I typically use InstantDomainSearch.com and LeanDomainSearch.com. The first one shows me real time results of the words I type. The second lets me type in a word and it shows me domains available with that word in it. For example, I am working with a new client that hired my consulting company to create a mobile fitness app that motivates people to lose weight and get fit. They liked the word 'motivate' and 'fitness', but obviously we can't use those words. Using the above mentioned tools I came up with names like GymSpark.me as the domain name, as in Gym Spark ME! You want to have a long list of potential names; in this case I came up with roughly 20 to 30 names. Then you want to decide the name with your whole team. You can use a survey, or just have everyone choose a name on a Google spreadsheet that you share with everyone.

A common rule of thumb is to always try to come up with a short name. The shorter a website or app name, the better. If you look at all of the famous companies out there, they are short and simple, usually one or two words. Amazon, eBay, Facebook, Snapchat, Uber, AirBnB, Slack, Twitter, Pandora, Spotify, Tinder, and many more. As you see, they are all consistently short, simple, and easy to remember. Unfortunately, once you have a name, you still have to search on TradeMarkia.com to see if someone already has it trademarked. If you are lucky, then no one will own your name. If they do, then it's back to the drawing board (unless your idea is totally different). Now, if you have chosen a name that isn't already trademarked, you'll want to create a logo and figure out your company colors. I like to use DesignMantic.com as a resource to see a diverse set of logos in just a few seconds. All you have to do is type in your app name and the industry your market is in. You will see a ton of logo ideas, and although you may not like most of them, you might find some inspiration from one of them. Another good idea is to just go on Google images and look at different app logos. What about your favorite apps? What do they look like? I find that most app, website, or company logos are quite simple. Your goal is to try and encompass your industry and your core value in an eye-catching logo.

Creating a logo can sometimes be a very difficult task. You may want to create ten or more different versions of the same logo, with different colors, different placement of icons, or different shapes. This way you can send out a survey to your friends, family, and peers to ask which one they like the most. Once you have decided on your logo and have checked the availability of the trademark, you can start branding everything that you create. This includes your surveys, newsletters, website, mobile app, business cards, marketing materials, or anything that you show people or give people. Having a brand, logo, name, colors, and everything that goes into your company identity helps boost morale in your startup. Facebook is known for its thumbs up icon, and YouTube its play button. Most companies have created their branding strategy around their core value; now it's your turn.

Beta Launch

If you have done everything correctly, you should be ready for your official beta launch. This means that you have an arsenal of test users, plenty of data, and an MVP that is everything the public wants. You can actually launch your website not just to your testers, but their friends and family, people on social networks, tech gurus, developers, and other startup founders. This is the most crucial period of your startup. You can either grow quickly and gain a lot of praise, or you can crash, burn and wither away just like the other thousands of startups that do every day.

Once you make your website or mobile app live, whether you have to wait for approval in the app stores or simply have to push a button to make your website go live, your team should be closely monitoring everything: your server(s), analytics, database, heatmaps (if you are using them), email support, phone calls, etc. This is the time where your complete attention is needed for any emergencies, quick feedback from users, bugs, issues, problems, server crashes, and more.

If you are somehow lucky enough to get onto Product Hunt, this could mean an influx of journalists reaching out to you for stories, or a lot of people hitting your server(s). You need to make sure that your product stays up and running. Here are some of the things you should have prepared before you actually launch your beta:

- Press release
- Blog posts written and scheduled for the next few weeks
- Graphics & wording for social media
- Landing page with sign-up ready to go
- App store information and details along with graphics
- Plenty of email addresses with your domain name
- Your investor pitch deck
- Q & A ready for journalists

There are plenty of other things you can prepare beforehand, and I suggest you do as many as possible. Once you launch your beta you will be so busy that you simply won't have time to do less important things. Also, it's better to have documents with wording, descriptions, answers, and company wide information ready so that you can copy and paste it when the time comes. Your team should be in sync when it comes to wording, vision, and answers so that every time any member of your team talks to someone about the company, the result is consistent.

A good way to get your wording figured out is to write a press release. This holy grail of marketing documents is a way for you to do a few things. First, you will hopefully reach journalists who are interested in covering your story. Next you will be getting your content into the search engines so that when someone searches for keywords in your space, your press release will pop up. Lastly, you are officially establishing your launch date through the press release. Here's an example of a press release I wrote for Instamour back in 2014 (minus the fake phone number):

Contact:
Kristin LaSalle, Marketing & PR
Phone: (610) 555-1212
Email: feedback@instamour.com
Twitter: @instamour

Instamour Raises Capital in Seed Round and Wins Techie.com 100 Award

PHILADELPHIA - May, 19th 2014, Instamour, the developer of the cutting edge mobile video dating app of the same name, has secured $150,000 in seed money and was recently named on Techie.com's Emerging 100 Companies list for 2014. Instamour was honored with a place on this prestigious list as the company helps people form relationships in real time, safer and more securely than other dating platforms available today.

Instamour has been formally accepted as one of a handful of new tech startups to the StartFast accelerator program in Syracuse New York for the summer 2014 program. The designation provides $100,000 in funding including $25,000 for equity and a $75,000 convertible note. This adds on to the initial $50,000 Instamour received for a total of $150,000 raised in this seed round.

The Instamour team is currently seeking to close a round of at least $500,000 in the coming months to scale its business and gain critical mass. "We couldn't be more excited about investing in Instamour. We think it is a tremendous opportunity in a chronically underserved market," said Chuck Stormon, Managing Director of StartFast Venture Accelerator.

Instamour has been gaining ground and is attracting a significant user base both in the US and international markets. With over 65% of singles in America using dating apps, the industry is growing fast. The company has recently been featured at events in San Francisco, New York, Las Vegas, and Philadelphia and has users in over 20 cities, including New York, Washington DC, Philadelphia, Baltimore, Boston, California, and Chicago. Internationally they are present in Spain, France, Italy, UK, Turkey, Dubai, and countries in both Asia and the Middle East.

"When I first started building Instamour, it was before Vine and Instagram video had been released. I knew my technology was something that would be quickly adopted by people because this is truly the next evolution in mobile dating," said Jason Sherman, Instamour CEO. "Single people everywhere are looking for a real-time experience, and that is exactly what my team and I are providing them with."

Additionally, Instamour has recently hired several new team members including Joshua Nicholson, a full stack developer and Harvard University graduate, Meng-Yi Hsu, an iOS and Android developer from Columbia University, and Josh Detweiler, a user acquisition and globalization expert who formerly worked for MeetMe prior to its acquisition by QuePasa for $100 million. "What drew me to Instamour was the diverse team and how unique the idea was. I didn't need any convincing to join the team, especially since what they are doing is pretty game changing. Video is the future, and Jason was clever enough to realize that early on. Instamour's energy and passion shines brighter than most teams I have worked with in the past. I'm excited to grow with them and see this through to the end, " said Detweiler.

The app is free to use and is currently available on the iTunes App store as well as the Google Play marketplace.

As you can see, the press release is full of keywords, the value proposition, funding milestones, quotes from the founders, and marketing facts. This not only helps your team fully realize your position, but when people ask you about your company, you will know what to say. Seeing your answers written out helps you remember what they are. The last thing you want to do when an investor asks you a question is hesitate or stumble.

When you write your press release, your main goal is to make it newsworthy; that's why it is called a press release and not a blog release. It's meant for the press. So make sure it is full of facts, numbers are great, analytics and statistics are awesome, and funding milestones are good too. Don't forget that if you want to personally say something, put it in a quote. It's also great to get some quotes from your users, kind of like testimonials. Ultimately you want journalists to see this press release and be able to gather enough information that makes for a good story. They will most likely want to follow up with you to ask more questions, so be prepared.

The other thing that goes hand in hand with a press release is an email newsletter to your members. I always use MailChimp to send mine out. You want these to be nice and short. Every time you send out a newsletter with an update, it should grab the subscriber's attention. You do this by giving them something important that will keep them engaged with your company or your platform. You can see one I wrote for Instamour back in 2013 when we were first starting out and things were heating up.[9] Here it is without any formatting or images:

Dear Amours,

Thanks for being so patient; we have worked hard on the new interface and improving functionality and it is almost ready for you to see. Please share it with your friends, and leave us a 5 star review in the app store if you love it (which you will).

We have only been live on the App store for one month, but have been getting tons of feedback from you, and are happy to have thousands of downloads from around the world!

Some of the features we have been improving upon are: instant chat, video calling, creating videos, and other minor details. You will find the new interface easier to navigate, simpler to use, and more beautiful!

Also, this is exciting: We are a proud sponsor of the Q102 Jingle Ball 2013 Concert! So if you are local to Philadelphia, you can enter our contest to win free tickets and backstage passes; all you have to do is make a great Video Profile!

---

[9] http://newsletter.jasonsherman.org

If you aren't near Philadelphia, we could really use some more Videos on your profiles to show everyone how awesome Instamour is. We are going to grow very rapidly in the coming months, and we thank you for all of your support! :)

Create some videos, instant chat and video chat, and start meeting people!

If you have any questions, feedback, or just love us shoot us an email: feedback@instamour.com

In the meantime, follow us on all of our social networks below and check out our launch video!

This was one of our longer newsletter emails, but it was effective. We had a high click through rate, and more people uploaded videos to our platform. So it worked. I did notice that shorter emails had a higher click through rate than longer ones. Common sense will tell you that people don't like reading long emails, so grab their attention with something short yet full of useful information. Sometimes we would even throw in some industry statistics to spice things up a bit. As you send out newsletters, write a press release, and start distributing your content, you are slowly becoming a marketing expert in some ways. Content distribution is one of the key ways startups have succeeded in the past historically. If nobody knows you exist, then you aren't going to succeed. There are many ways of distributing content, I've told you just two so far. You don't need to hire a publicist or a PR firm this early on, as long as you do the same things they would do by yourself.

The most important resource every startup needs to have is a pretty simple one: a blog. Since you already have a server where you are hosting your website, you can very easily install Wordpress on your server on a subdomain such as blog.domainname.com. Choose a theme that goes with your company colors and market, add a couple widgets for social sharing and spam avoidance, and you are ready to write some great content.

There are a couple of rules that I like to tell entrepreneurs when it comes to writing blog posts:

1. Never write about your company
2. Research everything you're writing about
3. Mention other articles from journalists you like
4. Use a tasteful amount of keywords
5. Add a couple of fun (or relevant) images
6. Keep it SEO friendly (around 500 words)

The last thing someone wants to do is read a blog post that talks about the company itself. Instead, you want to focus on relevant topics in your industry, which shows that you are an expert. By providing useful information to your readers, they will subscribe to your blog and most likely follow you on social media, and potentially become a customer. Once you get good at producing content and start to gain traction with subscribers, you can start to mention journalists on social media.

You definitely want to use facts and statistics, or just industry specific keywords, to really bring in the eyeballs. By showing that you are well-versed in your industry, not only will you attract subscribers but also journalists who may want to use some of your information in one of their upcoming articles. By mentioning journalists on social media with specific articles in your mentions, they are more likely to build a relationship with you.

Getting a journalist to write an article about your company is extremely difficult, especially since they get pitched 1000 times a day. Instead of asking them to write an article about your company, just have a conversation with them to form a relationship. After tweeting back-and-forth a couple of times or sparking some witty banter via email, they are more likely to write an article about your company. Also, if you have shown an interest in their writing style, their content, and their philosophies about your industry, your chances double up.

The more you know about your space from researching it, the better your content will be. Knowing what drives news articles will help you figure out the best topics to write about. By finding those articles and reading them, you will begin to become even more of an expert in your market. This helps you when you are in conversation with peers, team members, investors, and anyone else who is curious about your startup. It's like reading a history book about war, and then going into battle; you will have tons of tactics and strategies to add to your arsenal.

Keywords are something that you need to know, for many reasons. One of them is because you need to know what drives visitors to your site via SEO. This also works in the app stores for keyword marketing. Of course, social media platforms such as Twitter rely heavily on keyword searches too. I'm not saying you should bombard your written content with keywords, but you want to tastefully place them at the right places. If you can replace a regular word with a keyword that is more searchable, go for it.

Here's some written content without enough keywords:

Tons of companies are fundraising online through websites that let friends and family pitch in. More people are building new products every day thanks to these sites.

Here is that same content with plenty of keywords:

Tons of startups are raising money online through websites like Kickstarter that let friends, family, and the tech community pitch in. More than ever, entrepreneurs are building innovative, new gadgets every day thanks to these crowdfunding sites.

As you can see, I added a bunch of keywords that are not overly conspicuous. Another thing that goes hand in hand with keywords are images. Images are great because when you share your posts on social media; the platform usually grabs whatever image is available on the post. So instead of it grabbing something that is not relevant to your article, like a Wordpress logo, or your own logo, it will preferably grab something funny that catches the reader's attention. I like to use Internet memes often because they make people laugh, which causes them to click on my articles and read them. Also, if you throw another image or two in between paragraphs, it breaks up the reading a little bit and possibly makes them laugh again. Or if for some reason they can't finish reading the article at that moment, at least they know that they can pick up where they left off, right after the image they saw...kind of like a fun bookmark.

Videos are just as powerful as images, if not more so. With a video, you are capturing someone's complete attention, both aural and visual. Make sure your video is short, and compelling to watch. If not, they will click off and go watch a cat video instead. A good product video has helped many startups succeed. You may or may not have seen the Dollar Shave Club video that sparked huge growth in the company. Go ahead and Google it....I'll wait. The video was part of an intense marketing campaign that helped bring in $65 million in revenue in just two years. Dollar Shave Club was just acquired for $1 billion by Unilever. It all started with a smart and funny video. I've created many videos like these for various products of mine, even a couple of parodies.

When producing a video you want to keep a couple of things in mind. First, people have a short attention span, so you want to grab them in the first 15 to 30 seconds. Secondly, you have to add a comedic element to your product (if you can). If your platform helps low income families get food from sustainable local farms, then comedy might not be the best choice. You can still create a compelling video with dramatic elements that will cause people to want to support your platform. Either way, you have to grab their attention with a call to action that is hard to resist. A minute and a half is a good starting point for your video, but it can be longer. I would suggest keeping it under three minutes if possible; any longer and you start to lose your audience.

You can use a screen capture tool like SnagIt.com to make a video of your screen while you are talking. That way you can show your platform in action. For mobile videos, I use software on my computer and plug my phone through my USB port to show my mobile app in action. It's always better to show your actual product in use, rather than a click-through mock up demo. I would suggest doing a professional voice over with a good microphone rather than your webcam. If you don't have access to one, find someone who does. Good audio and video quality can make or break your final video. You can go in many different directions when making a video, whether using a green screen, overlaying graphics, a cinematic approach, or just something simple. Just remember, whatever you do in your video, keep your target market in mind. What would they like to see?

Once you are done making your video, writing your blog posts, press release, and other content, it's time to post everything on social media. My suggestion is to post your content anywhere and everywhere. Here are some of the places I like to post my content:

- Facebook (fan pages, groups, personal page)
- Twitter
- Google+ (personal pages, community pages)
- Pinterest
- StumbleUpon
- Reddit
- Digg
- YouTube
- Hacker News
- Blogs
- Forums
- Messageboards

Another great place to post your startup if you are looking for extra exposure is on BetaList.com. Additionally, you should spend the time to fill out profiles on Angel.co and Gust.com, because both of these platforms are used regularly by investment companies. These platforms will require you to add every piece of information about your company. If you use F6S.com, you can use your profile to sign up for accelerators, contests, and submit your info to investors. Some investment companies only accept submissions from these sites, so it's a good rule of thumb to fill them out before you start fundraising. You can also promote your startup on Craigslist, especially if you are looking for interns. All you have to do is repurpose your written content to cater to a more ad-like appearance. Mention that you are looking for people to help you test your platform or product, and that there is a possibility of employment if they do well. Posting content in a variety of places such as the ones I listed (especially the public ones), will help the content show up in more search results when people look up keywords in your industry. You are essentially getting free SEO while pushing your content.

A fun way to engage your target audience and give people an incentive is to host a contest. There are virtually a billion different ways you can run a contest. You can give away cash or big prizes, tickets to a concert, a meet and greet with a local celebrity, a trip to an island or Disneyworld, and anything else you can think of that is related to your industry. People love winning things, so it's a win-win for you and them. You get new users to sign up to your platform or buy your product, and they get the chance to win a new Xbox, or a trip to the Bahamas. Either way, contests are fun, and usually don't cost a lot, especially if you can get a sponsor to foot the bill. Look up local restaurants, businesses, and companies that have a ton of money. Here in Philadelphia, companies like Comcast sponsor events all the time. You can also give out custom Bitly links to people to help you promote the contest, and can compensate them based on how many clicks and/or signups you get from them.

You should always use Bitly to track how many people are clicking on your links. When it comes to marketing your beta, just make sure everything you do gives you some type of measurable result. If not, stop doing it immediately or change the way you are doing it. Also, don't forget to make sure you have graphics on all your posts so that they are visually appealing. Remember to use keywords, because that way more people find your content when they do searches. Once you are posting content on a regular basis you should start to see some results in your data. Analyzing this data is something that you should do every day, and it helps you make better decisions not only on how and where to post your content but how to run your business overall. Analytics are the backbone to every startup.

Analytics

With so many tech startups popping up every day, it's no surprise that there are an increase in analytics startups as well. Big data and infrastructure technologies are the hottest thing around in the tech world. Even a local analytics company I am close to and have written stories about was recently acquired by a larger company. So what exactly does an analytics company do that is so valuable in this day and age? Quite simply, they collect and store data, gain insights from it, and then help you turn those insights into real value for your startup. I like to call analytics the foundation to data driven decision making. As I mentioned in an earlier chapter, you shouldn't be making decisions on a whim. Let the data tell you what moves to make.

You may have heard that your KPIs (Key Performance Indicators) will help you determine which pieces of your platform are achieving the results you are looking for. One way to figure out your KPIs is by using SMART criteria:

- Specific – target a specific area for improvement.
- Measurable – quantify or at least suggest an indicator of progress.
- Assignable – specify who will do it.

- Realistic – state what results can realistically be achieved, given available resources.
- Time-related – specify when the result(s) can be achieved.

I personally don't use KPIs or the SMART system, and most techies will say that it is an antiquated model. We like to use the term "key metrics," and important numbers like CPA (Cost Per Acquisition). Your key metrics are the vital pieces of data that drive the success of the company. That could mean a variety of things. For example, here are some key metrics that I kept track of over the years:

- How many visitors created a profile
- How many users paid $.99 to unlock more videos
- How many items did a user list to sell within a 30 day period
- How many messages did one user send per day
- How many videos did each user upload per month
- How many customers went past the free trial to actually start paying for the platform

There are so many more I could list, but I think you get the idea. Your CPA is probably one of the most important numbers when you have a tech startup. Knowing your cost per acquisition will determine what your profit (if any) will be at the end of the day. If your CPA is $5, and a customer only spends $3 on your platform during the lifetime of their account, that could be a bad thing. There are rare instances where a loss in CPA is all right. In the early 2000s, PayPal famously gave away $10 to new customers for signing up, and existing ones got $10 for referrals. PayPal made billions in the long term, got acquired by eBay, and the rest is history.

Let's say your CPA is $5, and a customer spends $3 a day; your profit would be $85 for that user per month. If you can do that for 1,000 users, then you will be making $85,000 per month. It's highly unlikely, but hey, shoot for the stars! There's a nifty little CPA calculator on Clickz.com that I like to use.[10] Your end goal should be to make sure that your CPA or CPC (Cost Per Conversion) will be lower than the marketing dollars you spent getting them. Your CPC is also important because that will determine on how much it cost you to get a customer who's actually purchasing something on your platform. You might find this number to be higher because maybe only 10% of your acquired users are purchasing something on your platform. When less people are spending money, your CPC becomes higher. You have to use formulas, preferably in a spreadsheet, to determine your CPA and CPC.

The fun part in analytics is when you get to make decisions based on the data you are compiling. There's a

---

[10]http://cpa.jasonsherman.org

cool little trick I like to use when determining if people are willing to spend money on certain features. Survey results will only get you so far. People may say they will spend $5 a month to upgrade their profile, but how many of them will really pay the $5? Without building the actual functionality to purchase something, accept payments, and everything that goes along with that, you can simply have a button that says "Unlock for $5". When somebody clicks the button, an alert will appear saying 'Thank you for letting us know you would like to unlock this feature, we will notify you as soon as this feature is available'. This will give you a metric telling you how many people are willing to actually pay the $5 for that feature. I know this isn't the same thing as actually getting the sale, but it's close enough.

There are many micro experiments, A/B testing, and other growth hacks you can use to help determine the results you're looking for. Say you have 1000 beta users. To make this simple, half of them are in Europe, and half of them are in America. You can send the half in Europe a certain version of your mobile app, and the other users in America a different version. You gather the data based on their behavior, and then switch versions. By using this method of A/B testing, you will find different data among different demographics. This will help you make decisions on what features are more popular in different parts of the world. You may find that certain features work better in Europe, the Middle East, or Asia, than in America. Either way, there are an unlimited number of experiments you can run to get great data and metrics.

Once you get the results you want, you can iterate your platform based on the data. You might even realize that your platform features are so vastly different in certain markets that you are better off building standalone apps just for those markets. For example, let's say you are building a fitness app. Users in Europe may be a little less social at the fitness clubs whereas here in America, they like to work out in groups and challenge each other. So you release a version in Europe that is more about personal goals, and the one you launch in America features group challenges. Once you get enough data, you can determine if it's working out this way. If you swap versions with countries, you may actually be shocked with some of the results. You might find that Europeans like to challenge each other more than Americans. Either way, it's smart to try different tests to make sure that you are analyzing the right data and results.

If you were painting a mural for a client, analytics would be the colors the client chose for you to paint it with. They took the decision away from you and made your life easier. That's the fundamental piece of analytics that you should grasp. You shouldn't be making decisions on a whim; you should be making them based on data. This holds true even more so when you are implementing monetization and revenue strategies into your platform. One of the most difficult things I've had to do in my startups is determine what feature I should add monetization to. Depending on what market you are in, revenue is the most important thing you will need to add to your platform. I'll get more into that when we reach the investor chapter. A great rule of thumb when running your startup is that if you can earn enough revenue per month to cover your monthly expenses, then you have a perfectly viable business model.

Typically, if you are running a social platform, revenue isn't the sole focus; user acquisition is. The issue with this is that without earning revenue, you will almost always need to seek outside funding in order to scale your platform. Again, in certain markets this is the way to go, but in others it isn't. The same way you test features with various demographics is the same way that you test monetization. A lot of entrepreneurs struggle with monetization because they simply cannot think of creative ways to implement a revenue model in their platform. This is why they almost always fall back on advertising, which is a mistake.

Advertising only works when you have a large pool if users, typically in the 1 million or more range. If you only have say 100,000 users, you are not generating enough eyeballs, clicks, or views to merit a decent ad revenue. Also, implementing ads early on will upset your small user group because they really don't want to be bombarded by ads; they just want to use your product. On the other hand, if you think about which feature (or features) are most valuable to your users, there are definitely creative ways to earn a bit of revenue.

The first thing you want to do is go back to your core value proposition. Let's say that your core value proposition is the ability to snap a picture of something broken, and people who know how to fix it will respond to you with a price on how much they can fix it for and how soon they can get it done. Let's assume that your app is free, and that you have roughly 100,000 users. You also might have a couple of hundred service providers. You can probably start charging a small fee to your service providers for giving them these jobs. In the beginning, you may want to make this service free to get people to start using the app. But after gaining some real traction and engagement, there's no reason you can't charge something for the value you are providing. So instead of putting ads on your platform after you start to see some traction:

Try thinking of creative ways you can monetize your user base tastefully.

Another thing entrepreneurs always tell me they plan on doing when they first start building their platform is that they are going to partner with larger companies. Please stop saying this. Seriously, it's not going to happen early on. Why would a large company partner up with a tiny company who doesn't even have a platform built, doesn't have any traction, and doesn't have any revenue? They won't, unless you have a family connection, or are the luckiest person in the world. Partnerships often happen years after proof has been made that your platform or product holds value in the marketplace. So focus on traction and revenue before your focus on partnerships.

In my opinion, even though revenue is a great thing to have, user engagement is much more important. You can be making $10,000 a month on your platform, but if your users are not engaging enough, and that user engagement is not growing, then that means you probably won't be able to scale your platform. If you can't scale your platform, that means you pretty much have a lifestyle business. Either that or you need to hire new talent to help you figure out ways to engage your audience at a higher level. One of the most popular ways of engaging your audience nowadays is through Gamification. Gamification is pretty much what it sounds like - making your platform more like a game, so that people feel as though they are winning something, earning points, or challenging their friends.

In one of my earlier tech startups, we gave users the ability to earn points for doing certain things on the platform. Some of these actions were:

- Starting a group with friends
- Inviting new users to your groups
- Redeeming a coupon
- Sharing an event on various social media platforms

- Completing their profile
- Meeting with a group at the same location

We also gave out points in tiers or levels. So if you did something 10 times, you would earn a certain amount of coins, and the more you did, the more you earned. Those points translated into actual money, because if they had to unlock something on the platform, and they had to pay money to do so, they would just use points instead. Just like a video game, you would earn points and use them to unlock certain features instead of paying money for them. With the videogame industry being close to $100 billion in revenue in 2016, it's no surprise that gaming is a part of everyday life.

As an example, the hottest game right now, *Pokémon GO*, has done a couple of things using Gamification. It has created a virtual environment where people can now go outside and use augmented reality to play a game, challenge their friends, and socialize with new people. If you want more items (like Pokeballs), or you want to unlock other features, you have to pay for them. You can also earn them through the game. But with a $10 million per day revenue total, it's obvious that people are paying for items in the game just as much as they are earning them. You can easily implement something similar in your platform if you think of creative ways to engage your users while monetizing them at the same time.

Imagine you are in a room full of investors pitching your platform. They start asking you questions about your users, their demographics, their engagement, and your revenue. You should be able to spit out a mouthful of critical data that you've gotten from your analytics that goes something like this:

Our most engaged users are 25 to 34 years old, and live in New York, New Jersey, and Philadelphia. They are 62% male and 48% female. They spend 21 minutes, and $1.24 on average every day on our platform. 32% of our users come back within a week of using the platform to use it again. 28% of our users come back after 30 days to use it again. Our userbase has been growing 8% month over month, which shows tremendous user growth. Our CPA is $2.74 on average, and our LTV (lifetime value) per user is $43.16. Our data proves that we have amazing margins. Furthermore, with your investment, we can scale this to where we will earn $20 million over the course of the next three years.

If you can say something like that to a room full of investors, then you have done everything correctly up until now. Crafting your story, and pitching to investors comes with practice. I have pitched to well over 500 investors in various industries, different parts of the country (and the world), with a variety of results. The next chapter will teach you how to do the same.

Your Pitch

The Online Dating industry has been around for decades, yet it hasn't changed one bit. Dating sites still use the ubiquitous profile picture and static text information. More often than not, what you see isn't always what you get. But with Instamour's unique real time video platform, what you see is EXACTLY what you get.

Dating apps always use algorithms to match people. Really? Computers are effective at matching people? I don't think so. Since the beginning of time, humans have shown that they are good at matching themselves.

Even though dating sites haven't changed over the years, they HAVE changed in usage and value. Tinder is leading the pack and worth billions. Plenty of Fish was just acquired for $575 Million by dating leader IAC. And another market that is even bigger is the video market. With Snapchat being worth $25 Billion, and Twitter acquiring both Vine and Periscope for millions before even launching, it's no secret that the video market is growing rapidly. This is why Instamour is such a unique platform, integrating real time video technology into our safe and easy to use dating platform.

So you're probably asking yourself, "Why hasn't this been done before?" Well, the technology is new.

iPhones are only 8 years old and camera technology is relatively new also. When I came up with this idea back in 2004, the technology simply wasn't available. When Vine was released, we were already building Instamour, so we were right in the hotspot during 2012 / 2013. We continued to iterate and build out our platform until 2015, and this is what we built:

Video Demo Plays here

The platform you just saw was the subject of a provisional patent that we filed in the spring of 2014. Contingent on funding, we plan on further protecting our platform by filing a utility patent. Now you've heard it from me, but we have worked with so many colleges in the past 2 years that I thought it would be great if you could hear what they have to say about Instamour. We've worked closely with students and classrooms from the leading universities in Philadelphia and they've presented their findings to us in presentations. They performed surveys, consumer market research, analytics, user experience testing, and more to help us understand what we needed to build for our Version 2.0. We learned what people like and don't like about our app, which helped us build the best version that we could based on that data.

All the testing and launches we did were based on our first version, which we launched in September of 2013 for iPhone and January 2014 for Android. We used all of that user feedback and worked on V 2 which we just launched last month. During all of our promotions and launches we were able to acquire 150,000 users with little to no marketing spend. This was due to being a part of the StartFast Accelerator in the summer of 2014, implementing growth hacking techniques, press and media attention, and our university presence.

Of course I didn't do this by myself. Instamour has an amazing team of entrepreneurs. We have over 100 years of experience combined. I myself have been a serial entrepreneur for over 10 years, and worked in IT for 20. I've also started and sold various businesses. Co-founder and CTO Evan Brophy has been a full stack of developer for 10 years and built the backend for our scalable platform. Kristin LaSalle, co-founder and VP of marketing, has worked with matchmaking companies, Fortune 500 companies, is a master of sales and she knows how to get in touch with our market. Eric Raymond who is on our Board of Directors, is also Chairman of Business Development. He's had multiple exits, is a Wharton graduate, and has tons of experience and connections. We also have several other members on our team who help us with awareness, branding, international relations, user acquisition, relationship coaching, and we also have a ton of interns from local area universities.

Our Board of Directors has had many exits, raised and managed hundreds of millions of dollars in funding, and has helped us choose the right paths to succeed.

As we scale our user base further and implement industry standard proven monetization methods, based on our actual data from the past year, we can earn $20MM in 2 years, with half being from in-app purchases such as upgrading your profile videos from 4 to 10 or sending introductory video messages to other members. The other half would come from monthly subscriptions which would unlock all the features and personal moderators which help members avoid inappropriate content or harassment. If each purchaser spends $15 per month engaging with matches for four months, that's $60, as opposed to one bad date that can cost $60. You can see more detail as well as positive revenue in our annual forecast.

This is why we are raising $1 million. Not to build our platform. Not to prove our concept. Not to run tests and experiments. We've already done all that. We are raising $1 million simply to scale our already built platform and already substantial user base to over 1M users in 12 months.

In the spring time we sat down with the leader in dating apps IAC because they asked us to come to their headquarters in New York City to have a sit down. They were impressed with our platform and loved what our platform offers. They only asked that we scaled our user base to over 1 million users and implement our monetization techniques. They want a second meeting after we accomplish those tasks. This is why we are here asking for your support - so we can reach those milestones and be added to the IAC portfolio or other acquirer in the dating space. Thank you so much for your time, I'd love to answer any questions you may have.

Now that's how you pitch a room full of investors. I actually recorded the above pitch where I presented in a room full of 200 investors[11]. When you are preparing your script or your pitch, generally you have an idea who your audience is. I always create multiple presentations, one for an older crowd, one for a younger crowd, one for investors in my industry, one for investors that are not in my industry, one to present in person, and one to email out to investors. The bottom line is that you always have to come prepared.

One of the many things I learned about investors is that they get pitched hundreds of times every single day. So they really want you to grab their attention from the get-go. If you can do that, then you will have their attention for the remainder of the pitch. Also, if you get a lot of questions at the end of your presentation this can be both a good and a bad thing. The reason I say this is because if they're asking you a lot of questions at the end of your presentation, it's not so much that they are interested as much as you may not have answered their questions in your presentation.

---

[11] http://investorpitch.jasonsherman.org

That's when things get more interesting. By answering most frequently asked questions in your presentation, not only will they find you to be an expert and more prepared, but you will find a more unique set of questions that you don't have in your presentation. This helps you answer questions that you might not have thought about originally, which actually helps you in the long run. For example, you might mention how many users you have on your platform, and how much revenue you earn from them. But maybe you don't mention how much content they upload to your platform. That's a question one investor asked me, 'How many videos do your users upload every day to your platform?' Believe it or not, at that particular time, I didn't know the exact answer. I just guessed so that I wouldn't look bad. But you should never do this, because if they truly are interested in investing in your product, they are going to find out eventually, and they may not like the answer they find. You might have just lost that investor.

One of the smartest things you can do after you're done a presentation and you get a question that you're not sure the answer to is write it down on your phone or on a piece of paper. If you have pitched as many investors as I have, you will end up with a pretty long list of questions. Your job is to answer them to the best of your ability. You want to know these answers like the back of your hand. If you are able to answer practically any question about your business without any hesitation at all, you will succeed.

As for your actual presentation, whether using PowerPoint or Keynote, you can always add a bunch of answers to the end of your presentation after the final slide. You never have to show them; they are there as a backup. We'll talk more about that in a minute. But for now I'm going to cover what your presentation should consist of. There are roughly ten points that you should hit when creating a presentation. Here they are in the order I prefer:

1. Problem
2. Solution
3. Market Size
4. Business Model
5. Competition (or Testimonials)
6. Marketing Plan
7. Team
8. Traction / Projections
9. Current Status
10. Needs

You might find variations of this on the Internet. Many people will tell you that the "perfect" presentation will look different. I'm just giving you my style based on the experience of pitching hundreds of investors. When you fill in these points with words (your script), it's no different than a sales pitch or a movie script. You're trying to get the audience to believe in you. There's a very creative way to include numbers and analytics, market statistics, and other typically boring numbers in your presentation. The first thing you can do is make your presentation very visual, using catchy graphics and charts. If you can make your audience laugh, even better. If you watched my video, you'll notice the whole room started to laugh in the beginning of my pitch. Boy does that break the ice and allow you to breathe a little easier.

Once you have their attention, you start by telling them the problem that you are facing, which typically causes them to laugh because they feel your pain. Then your solution and how you plan on stopping this from happening again. If for any reason you forget the information that you're supposed to say on a slide, just improvise and keep going. Nobody will know any different because they didn't know what your script said in the first place. I've done this quite a few times and it works. A lot of entrepreneurs tell me that they get nervous when they stand in front of people and they freeze up. This happens to everybody, even experts. This is why you have to practice as much as possible. There are a couple of other tricks you can use.

The first thing I do besides practicing my pitch, is concentrate on my breathing. Breathing deeply before a presentation helps you calm down. Sometimes a shot of liquor helps too...seriously ;). Over time I realized that with a couple of minor tweaks to your delivery, eye and body movement, you can work wonders in front of a large crowd. For example, you want to look at a certain place in the crowd for at least two seconds before you turn your head away. It shows that you are able to connect with your audience and they're able to look at you while you speak to them before you turn away. Another thing you can do if you don't like seeing people stare at you, is to simply look at their ears. I know that sounds silly, but it works. They will think that you are looking at them, and you won't get nervous by staring at their eyeballs. I used to do this in the past and it always works. Don't forget to slow down. People have a tendency to talk really fast when they are presenting. Just breathe, and take your time.

Some people naturally don't have stage fright, it's rare but it does happen. Assuming you aren't one of those people, then try some of my tricks and see if they work. It goes without saying, you need to practice your presentation in front of the mirror so that you can see how your body moves, how you move your hands, your pacing, your breathing, and your delivery. Of course you should also practice in front of family and friends so that you can get feedback constructive and criticism. One of the things I like to do when I speak in public, and now in my personal life, is to take deep breaths between sentences, especially with words that I want to emphasize. Say the following sentences at your normal speaking pace without pausing:

In 2015, we launched our mobile app, and within a couple of months we were able to acquire 10,000 users. After graduating the accelerator program, we now have well over 100,000 users, and we are projected to reach 1 million users by the end of 2017.

Now say the following, twice as slow as you normally do and with all of the pauses and directions I give you:

In 2015, we launched our mobile app.
(head / eye shift, breathe / pause)
Within a couple of months we were able to acquire -
10,000 users (say this slowly).
(head / eye shift, breathe / pause)
After graduating the accelerator program,
(head / eye shift, breath / pause)
We now have well over 100,000 users,
(head / eye shift, breath / pause)
and we are projected to reach - **1 million users (say this slowly)** by the end of 2017.

See what a difference a couple of eye and head movements, deep breaths, and emphasis does? As you present to an audience, you are baiting them with emphasized words, especially if your visuals on the screen really move along with your rhythm. That's very important; it almost needs to be like a movie. Your slides should flow with your words. Your main goal when presenting in front of investors is to have them see your vision, believe in your goals, and make them want to be a part of it. One of the things I love after giving a presentation is having various investors walk up to me and tell me that they have gone through the same problem. That they feel my pain. That they want to be a part of my solution. Unfortunately, this doesn't usually translate into a check from an investor.

One last thing you have to practice, is your Elevator Pitch. This is a 30 second pitch that you should be able to say to an investor while sharing an elevator. Make it simple, use a couple of keywords, mention your pain point, your solution, and finally your vision. Here's an example of the elevator pitch I've given for Instamour thousands of times:

Instamour helps people see and hear someone's personality before meeting. Picture and text profiles just don't work anymore. With video profiles, instant chat, video messaging, and live audio or video calling, Instamour is the next evolution in mobile dating. Form real relationships in real time without ever having to send another email or disclosing any personal information and giving up your privacy.

Everyone who has ever heard this 30 second pitch understood Instamour's disruptive core value proposition immediately. Safety and convenience. Now it's your turn to write a 30 second pitch. Feel free to send me your pitch when you do at: http://Pitch.JasonSherman.org

Fundraising

Fundraising is by far the most time consuming and frustrating part of running a tech startup. Unfortunately it is a necessary evil. This is why time and time again I tell entrepreneurs to do as much as they possibly can without raising money. Investors are very slick when it comes to saying no. Try to keep in the back of your mind that they rarely say yes. Here are some of the things investors might say to you:

- I'm interested in your platform
- I would like to talk to you some more
- Send me your deck
- I'm interested in investing in your company
- I might be interested in working with you
- Great presentation, you are on the right track
- You should talk to 'so and so'
- Your company would work great with one of my portfolio companies
- Let's talk in 6 months
- I'd like to see more data
- Shoot me an email and let's go from there

The list goes on and on. The way I see it, until an investor physically writes you a check, and that check clears into your bank account, everything is a no. I've been promised by many investors, many times that they were going to fund one of my startups, and they never did. Sure, there were a lot of back-and-forth emails, phone calls, documents being sent over, questions being asked, but in the end they didn't invest in my companies. Also, keep in mind that investors don't sign an NDA. They simply are pitched by way too many companies to waste time signing them. They are not going to steal your idea, but they may fund it. Another reason that they cannot sign them, is because they may be working with a startup already that is similar, and therefore they would be immediately violating the terms of the NDA.

Some investors don't even plan on investing in your company, but they want to meet you to see if you can help them. I'll never forget the time when a potential investor asked me to go to lunch with him to find out more about Instamour. He said he was interested in investing. So I brought my laptop, did a quick PowerPoint pitch for him, and he said he was impressed. Then he quickly changed the conversation to tell me about an idea he had for an app. He asked me what I thought about it. I told him it was a good idea, but it would take a decent amount of time and money to build and market it. When he asked me how much it would take and how long, I told him. He then asked me if I would be willing to build it for him. I quickly realized that the meeting was not for the purpose of discussing my company, but to discuss his idea.

When he asked me if I would do it for equity, I told him the only way I would do it is if I got paid cash. Obviously, we never ended up working together. Truth be told, I wasn't planning on building the idea with him in the first place. I was disappointed that he totally downplayed Instamour and instead just wanted to know if I would build his app. The shocker for me was that when the check came for lunch, he actually made me pay for half. After that, I was asked by other investors to meet for a potential investment in my company. Again, based on my experience, intelligence, creativity, and knowledge about the tech industry, they asked me to help them with their idea. Some asked me to run their tech startup, others to help them build their app. So you need to watch for those types of investors as well. Once this happened a few times, I started to simply ask investors if they were willing to offer me a term sheet before meeting. Once you are offered a term sheet and you have it in your hands, that is the first step to getting funding from the investor.

Even when you get a term sheet, which is a pretty big deal in the tech world, that is still technically a no. A term sheet is what it sounds like: a document an investor gives you that spells out the terms of the investment. I had a term sheet for one of my previous companies that said we were raising $600,000. Two months into the funding round we had roughly three quarters of the money committed. One of the major investors who promised to fund us (many times) pulled out at the last minute (literally), and the whole deal fell apart. So even when you have a term sheet, it still means no. I can't tell you how many times I've been told that the hardest part about raising money is convincing a lead investor to give you a term sheet (and sign it). Ironically, it's usually an investor who says this.

Getting investors to fill your round is actually the hard part. In my example, it caused me to be in a state of limbo. I was constantly being distracted by pitching to investors and trying to fill the rest of the round so that I could have successfully taken my business to the next level. The problem with fundraising is that while you are pitching investors, preparing documents, and going through the due diligence process, you are being distracted from running the business. Of course you will still do everything it takes to make the company succeed, but without the funding, you will continue to do it in bootstrap mode, which is minimal at best. Investors like to see the founders of a tech startup running the company full time. Most entrepreneurs I work with run their startups full time for at least a year, and can probably do it for another six months to a year, for a total of two years without a paycheck. Try living without a paycheck for 2 years, and get back to me with how easy that is.

This is a major Catch-22. You need funding to scale your business, but investors want you to scale your business before they give you funding.

Sometimes they just flat out tell you that they don't invest in your industry. This is something that you should pay attention to in a really big way. When an investor tells you that they don't invest in your industry, you should find out which one they do invest in. This can help you in a variety of ways. You should be keeping track of all the investors you have spoken to in a spreadsheet. Here's the information I keep track of:

- Full name
- Investment company name
- Email
- Phone number
- Referral (if any)
- What industry they invest in
- What stage company they invest in
- How much they usually invest
- Portfolio companies

By keeping track of this you will always know which investors to target. If they keep telling you that they invest in veterinary platforms instead of family doctor platforms, then maybe you should build a vertical, or even pivot your startup. Here's a trick I've used to gauge an investor's true interest when they tell me they don't invest in my industry but they do invest in something similar. I respond by simply saying that I had included that concept in my business plan, and that I had intended to build something along those lines once I've raised money and reached scale with my current platform. This may or may not interest them. But at least you know that you are now on their radar.

If you actually decide to pivot your startup or build a vertical, then at least you know you have the right investors that might be interested in investing in your new platform. It also helps when you have friends who have startups, because although the investor didn't want to invest in your startup, maybe they'll want to invest in your friends' startups. Cold emails or cold calling never really work. A warm introduction to an investor almost always helps a new startup. Here's an example of an email I wrote to many investors with a tech billionaire's endorsement:

Dear Investor:

I was referred to you by (tech billionaire's name), who thought you'd be interested in what we're doing and how we are changing the way people form relationships...

We have a fast-moving, young company named Instamour where we have developed a unique way for people to form real relationships in real time – which is what billions of people have been waiting for. By leveraging the latest developments in communications, media, and technology, we are taking human interaction to the next generation by eliminating obsolete picture and text based relationship profiles and replacing them with real-time video communications. By doing this, our platform shatters the legacy technology communication barrier that has plagued the multi-billion dollar online dating market for decades.

Our community doesn't search old, static text and photos for someone they think they might like – instead they experience real people in real time from "moment one," which is how real relationships really work. By harnessing the power of real time video and communication in the mobile paradigm, our users get an in-depth experience with a potential relationship immediately and securely...anytime, anywhere. This richer experience creates real relationships and is revolutionizing the way people begin to engage.

The bottom line is that we have pioneered the next generation way of creating a real relationship using today's technology. We're addressing a massive market that is plagued with antiquated platforms, and the opportunity in front of us is killer. I'd love to spend a few minutes talking about our strategies with you – would you have some time to talk this week, possibly Thursday afternoon?

As you can see, this email starts off with my mention of the investor, and quickly grabs their attention with a one-liner. Emails without an introduction from someone rarely get noticed. Investors are flooded with requests. Truth be told, what I tell entrepreneurs every day is that they shouldn't be wasting their time reaching out to investors anyway. Instead, I tell them to work as hard as possible to reach what I like to call - the four T's:

1. Technology
2. Team
3. Traction
4. Turning a profit

When you sit down with an investor, these are typically the four main things they look for before they consider writing a check. When it comes to technology, they want to know that you have built an MVP that is already scalable, can handle the influx of millions of users, and that you have used best practices to build it. They are always going to ask you what your differentiator is as well. Why do people prefer your platform over others, and what have you done to ensure that others can't copy you that quickly. Keep your answers short but detailed.

As for infrastructure, you'll want to make sure your database and platform is hosted on a scalable server such as AWS or Rackspace. You should have API documentation fully written out to explain your platform to anyone who is interested. You should have technical documentation, mock-ups, clickable demos, and your actual platform available to show in front of investors at any given time. Always be prepared to show your product. You should be one button push away from showing it. Investors don't have patience, and they hate when a technology company can't show their technology quickly. Ever go to a restaurant and wait an hour for your food? I'll bet you didn't go back to that place again.

If your technology is where it should be, you will be able to ensure investors that their money will not be going to build any of this, simply to scale it to the next level. I mean, you are a technology company overall, so your technology should be at the highest standard possible. Part of this means that your technology employees or cofounders should have the same high standards. Your CTO can come with you to meetings, but it's not necessary. Eventually, investors will want to meet your CTO and make sure that he or she knows their stuff. Investors sometimes ask questions regarding technology, and the CTO will be the one to answer them, but that doesn't mean that you, the CEO shouldn't know those answers also. As a matter of fact, when you first build your tech startup, as I said before, you will wear many hats.

Your team is just as important as your technology, because without your team, you are just a lone wolf with a great idea. Investors want to make sure that when they fund your company, your team is going to help you succeed. This means that each member of your team should have a special skill-set related to their title. So your VP of marketing should have tons of experience with both Fortune 500 companies as well as startups. They should be able to spit out information about your marketing plan without hesitation. If an investor asks you specific questions about your demographics, age groups, marketing budget, or advertising spend, your VP of marketing should know those answers like the back of their hand. Investors say that they invest in entrepreneurs, but it's more realistic to say that they invest in an entire team. If they don't feel confident that each member of your team is an expert in their field, then they will think that their money will go just down the toilet.

You need to make sure that every member of your team is on the same page as you. The vision has to be clear, the answers consistent, and everyone's skill should complement each other in some shape, way or form. If you don't feel confident in yourself and in your team, then an investor won't either. It's a great idea to have mock interviews with your team. Have a member of your board of directors or advisory board come into your office one day and ask you questions that investors would ask. Then they can critique your answers, body language, and delivery. I've done this many times in the past, and it helps greatly.

Having a solid technology built by an expert team is awesome, but it's still not enough in most cases. You can argue that if you build a technology like Google did in the 90s, you can gain rapid market share simply because of your unique algorithm. I agree with you, but defensible technology startups are just so hard to come by nowadays. Traction is the thing that will make or break your company. Also known as "stickiness," traction is how engaged your users are, and how fast you are growing. If Google didn't have early adopters using their search engine (and advertisers paying for those eyeballs), all they would have is a great search engine with nobody using it. The same thing is true for Facebook; their early traction at Harvard made them realize that they potentially had something huge. So they started to branch off into other universities, and the traction continued to grow. The goal of your startup, whether it is an analytics tool, a dog walking app, an e-commerce site, a B2B service, or anything else, is to show traction in order to prove that your core value is in demand by the market. By showing traction to an investor, they will immediately know that their funding will go towards scaling that traction to make it even bigger.

So you might be asking yourself, what kind of traction are investors looking for? The truth is, there are many variables that will determine this. For example, whereas my video dating startup has roughly half a million users, here in Philadelphia that doesn't mean anything. Whereas if I would move to Silicon Valley, that many users might make investors open their eyes a bit. Different cities and different investment communities look for different things. Some are excited about 100,000 users, some 1 million users or more. A 5% growth rate each month might be exciting to an investor in Texas whereas in New York, they may be looking for more of a 20% growth rate month after month. Either way, you need to know your city's investment community strategy, philosophy, and outlook on traction. If your startup would do better in another city, then you might have to make the tough decision to uproot your life and move your whole team out there. I decided to stay put in Philadelphia even though the investment community doesn't invest in the types of startups I have built over the years. So I had to raise money outside of Philadelphia, and it worked a few times. Ultimately, if you are living and working in the city where you are raising money, it will be a lot easier for you.

It's definitely safe to say, if you have been able to get 1 million users for a consumer platform, and it is growing at least 10% month over month, then you definitely will get the attention of investors. If you are able to get 250 or more customers for your B2B startup, and each of them is paying a monthly fee to use your platform, that is also some pretty good traction. As I have said before, your goal will always be to get as far as you can without investors' help. Because as soon as they see that you need money, they will know that they have an advantage over your company. You want to always have the upper hand, and not seem desperate for their funding.

If you can turn a profit by earning revenue so that your company is self-sufficient, that is the best position you can be in. Especially in a market where revenue is the number one factor in raising money, you should definitely include some form of monetization and show proof of revenue prior to raising a round. Let's say you want to build a consumer platform like Instagram, and your goal is to acquire a million users as quickly as possible. Maybe you are in Miami, Florida and investors there want to see revenue before they invest. Even a million users might not impress them, because they might think it's a gamble whether or not they will get their money back one day with a decent ROI (return on investment). In your mind, you may be thinking that if you had a million users, that you could add monetization later (think Facebook, Snapchat). This is a faulty line of reasoning; investors generally want to see that your company is already generating revenue before they will fund you.

Something you should be doing on a regular basis is writing your own answers to questions that you think investors will ask you. A good way to do this is to have your board of directors, advisors, mentors, peers, and even team members ask you questions. Once you write down the answers, go over them with the same people to see what they think. This part is mostly trial and error. Luckily, you can save a lot of this time by reading the questions investors asked me when I was raising money for Instamour back in 2014. Here are some of them:

Q: What is your biggest challenge?

A: Not acquiring the funding needed to scale the business.

Q: Do you consider your company a Lean Startup? Why?

A: Yes we do, because we continuously run micro experiments and use the data to make our overall decisions. We don't spend a lot of money to run these experiments, and our team is working on equity and not a salary. Everything we do is analyzed on a granular level.

Q: Do you have a business model canvas for us to review?

A: Yes we do (hand them a copy).

Q: What are the holes in your company?

A: The main hole we need to patch up is development. We lack a dedicated Android developer and are seeking one who shows as much passion for our platform as we do. Once we find him or her we will gladly have them join our team.

Q: Why is your team the one I should back and are they all full time? Do you have any missing key positions?

A: Over the past year and a half our team has proven that we are dedicated to work for sweat equity and we have produced amazing results. We continue to build out our platform, and gain users using our own resources. This alone shows true dedication and desire for success. My cofounders and I are full time. While we do take part time contract work to earn an income, we put the majority of the earnings right into our company to keep it growing while we fundraise.

Q: Your customer acquisition expert is part time, why is that not a serious problem? Does he have a non-compete agreement?

A: [Redacted name] has proven that his skills are not needed full time, as he has shown in the past 6 months working with our company. He continues to give us as much time as needed, whether phone, Skype, email, text, or meetings in person. He is always there to perform the task(s) needed to fulfill a goal on time. Every employee has signed an NDA & Consultant Confidentiality and Inventions Assignment Agreement.

Q: How do/did you come up with the value for your company?

A: We base our valuation on an average of industry standards in our space as well as where we are at in our team, growth, technology, user base, prior funding rounds, as well as our lead investors who have committed a third of our round on this value.

Q: What is your key differentiator and what are your barriers to competition?

A: Incorporating video into our platform is our key differentiator. By eliminating emails and static profiles and instead incorporating dynamic video profiles and live video chat, this on its own makes us stand out from the other dating sites out there.

Q: Why won't another big company simply build what you have in 3-6 months?

A: Because larger players in the space will have to decide whether or not they want to spend the time and resources to build something like our platform, or simply buy our technology and our team to help them grow over the next few years. They are focused on earning revenue from their current platforms and the time and resources it will take for them to build something similar to our platform is not cost effective. Plus they would then have to market a whole new platform, which takes tons of time and resources, when we have already done the hard work. So a partnership or an acquisition would be preferable to them.

Q: How do you get customers?

A: We gain customers in many different ways. One of our main methods is un-incentivized targeted paid user acquisition. We also use many forms of organic marketing, such as social media, blogging, targeted ads on Twitter, Facebook, Pinterest, StumbleUpon, and other social networks. We sponsor or partner up with larger events or companies in the area to get more geo-localized users to help spread the word and saturate centralized areas.

Q: What is your customer acquisition cost? Is this for an active or paying customer?

A: We have run many experiments and optimized CAC down to $0.09 cents for each international user and $0.35 cents for each U.S. user. This is for an active customer. We are in the initial stages of testing our monetization campaigns, so as we earn more revenue while scaling our platform we will be able to determine a much more feasible lifetime value.

Q: Will you always have to pay to obtain customers? Aren't you seeing any network effect from 100k users?

A: We believe that once we reach a "sweet spot" with our stage of development and UA methods, we will start to gain a substantial amount of organic growth whereas our revenue will outpace our spend. We are currently seeing growth with a minimal spend rate right now to the point that we feel confident we will always grow, with or without a large budget.

Q: What platforms are operational/planned? What kind of traction are you getting?

A: We are currently live on iPhone, Android, and the Web. We are getting roughly 80% of our users on the Web, and 20% on mobile. We foresee mobile growing more in the next 12 months while Web steadily continues to grow. We plan on focusing some of our efforts on converting our Web users to mobile as well. We have gone from 10k users to 100k in just a few months and continue to grow.

Q: How are you defining traction?

A: Any user who logs back into our site or app within 30 days and leaves a comment on a profile, pushes a heart, uploads a photo or video, watches a video profile, engages in instant chat, phone calls, or video calls, is how we define traction.

Q: How many total users? How many active users per platform? How do you define active?

A: We have over 300,000 users, of which 12% are active, with a higher percentage of active on mobile versus web. An active user is someone who logs back into our app or site a month after signing up and engages on at least one level of traction.

Q: How often does the same customer visit your site? How long do they stay?

A: At least once a week, an average of 3 to 5 minutes.

Q: Your web engagement level seems very low? Why can't you convert them to mobile? Why not focus on mobile?

A: Simply put, we have shown that we can acquire users at a high-level for Web, and are now in the process of implementing the conversion process with education, email campaigns, and other calls to action to help guide our users to mobile. With mobile acquisition costs being so high, we feel as though it will be more cost-effective to convert our members from Web to mobile while targeting both platforms simultaneously.

Q: How will you raise the engagement level?

A: By solidifying our development infrastructure and optimizing our UI and UX to cater to ease-of-use, and more video content, as well as further integrating gamification and user engagement techniques that we have planned.

Q: How will you monetize your customers? Do you have proof? Results of experiments?

A: We already have campaigns with Google AdSense and are showing positive results in revenue, as well as running experiments with in app purchases that we have implemented on our Android app. We will continue to run in app purchase experiments on iPhone and Android, unlock more features, implement pre-roll video ads, as well as a monthly subscription service in the next 12 months.

Q: What happens if we do not invest?

A: We will continue to run the company in bootstrapped mode with our own resources, while we continue to optimize our strategies and grow the company to the best of our ability.

Q: How will we make money?

A: We believe that we will earn revenue(s) to the point where we will be profitable in 2 to 3 years whereas we will be able to sustain the company without further funding. We also believe a larger player may find us attractive and will want to acquire us for a large sum to bring you a decent return on your investment.

Q: How do you define success for your company? If we ask each member of your team, will they say the same thing?

A: Success for us is a large user base enjoying the platform and the unique features it offers. The more organic growth and word-of-mouth marketing that we receive, the more successful we believe we will be. As we receive a lot of testimonials and customer feedback based on relationships they have created from our application - that is the truest kind of success we can attain. Financial success is always a part of the equation as well, although we see that as a secondary form of success. Our number one belief is that if our customers are happy, then we did our job well and the fruits of our labor will come back ten-fold financially.

Q: Will you be able to hire the resources you need in Philadelphia? Why don't you move to Silicon Valley or New York?

A: We feel as though team members who are located in New York can easily relocate here to Philadelphia, but if need be, and the need arises, we would move to a different location. Eighty percent of our team is here in Philadelphia, so we feel as though the last remaining members can easily relocate to Philadelphia, or commute from a different state.

These are word for word questions that were asked to me by various investors between 2013 and 2014. I thought about the answers carefully, wrote them out, and went over them with everyone involved with the company. After practicing the answers, I was able to answer investors without any hesitation. My earliest answers to investors were commonly wrong answers. Most entrepreneurs don't know that the words they choose to answer questions can mean the difference between getting funding or not. You want to avoid negative words. You might not even think they are negative words or phrases. Here are some of them:

- Unfortunately
- Until we get
- We haven't been able to
- We tried to do that
- The problem is
- The issue is

There are plenty of others, but I'm sure you get the idea. I always focus on the positive aspects of the answer. This will help you seem confident, which will in turn make the investor confident. Here's an example of a sentence using negative words and positive words.

Here's the question first:

How come you haven't been able to reach 1 million users on your own yet?

Negative Answer: Well unfortunately, we still haven't been able to raise the money we need for our marketing budget. The problem is that we can't pay our employees a salary, so they can only work nights and weekends which gives us very limited branding and awareness. Plus we don't have money to pay developers. Until we get funding, we will be stuck where we are.

That's an answer you might give to an investor. It's riddled with holes and red flags. Let's try it now with a positive twist:

Positive Answer: Actually, we feel as though reaching 300,000 users in less than two years is quite impressive considering our limited marketing budget. Furthermore, based on our projections, with your financial support, we will be able to reach 2 million users in a matter of 12 months. If you look at other startups in our space who also have limited resources, they don't have as many users as we have. Finally, they are not constantly mentioned in the press & media with fantastic branding and awareness like we have.

Basically, you want to emphasize your positives, the things that help you stand out, while throwing out numbers, and stating milestones and dates. Make the investor believe that you know exactly when you plan on reaching certain numbers and that with their support you can reach them. It also helps to know an investor's mindset. When I was at the peak of pitching investors, I would regularly read their blog posts. Investors like to write blogs. You will be able to read about their philosophies, investing guidelines, the types of companies they like the most, who they've invested in the past, and what they look for in an entrepreneur.

Another smart thing you can do to prepare yourself for investors is to research them on the Internet, both on LinkedIn, and their personal website (if they have one). Investment companies have a corporate website so that you can research their philosophies and their portfolio companies. If you don't feel as though your vision will be aligned properly, or that they don't invest in companies like yours, then why bother talking to them? I made this mistake early on, where I spoke to pretty much any investor that would take a phone call, answer my email, or meet me in person. More often than not, they would tell me that they don't invest in my industry but that if I ever launch an app in their industry to let them know.

Connecting with investors prior to meeting them is a very important thing. Just like journalists, you need to build a relationship with an investor before you start to talk about funding. Just because you see startups raise millions of dollars in funding in the news, that doesn't mean they raise that money overnight. It typically takes an average of six months or even longer to raise a round of funding. It's a very long, grueling process that takes away from your core mission of building and scaling your startup. Early on in my tech startup career I was given some pretty valuable advice by a big investor:

Don't ask for funding, ask for advice and feedback.

This was the smartest thing I was ever told by an investor. I immediately stopped asking for money, and instead started saying that I value their input, and I would like their feedback on our startup to see if we are moving in the right direction. When you tell them this, they feel as though they are going to be involved in your startup without having to sign a check. This eases the pressure off of them, and makes them more willing to help you. More often than not they will potentially offer you some guidance, or maybe sit on your advisory board, or maybe they will help you get partnered up with one of their portfolio companies. Either way, by asking for help, advice, and feedback, you will be on their radar, and they will see what you are made of. Also, with the pressure of money off an investor's back, they might actually find your company appealing to their portfolio. Once they realize that you aren't desperate for money and that you are doing everything correctly, they might invest anyway. Just remember one thing: Investors like to always feel that they are in control and that they have the upper hand.

Now, before you bother reaching out to an investor, you need to make sure that you're choosing the right one. As I mentioned before, you need to do your research. When researching investors, you will want to look at what industry you are in, and what stage you are in. For example, maybe your startup is in the on-demand, home-improvement space, and you are considered early stage. This means you want to look at investment companies that have funded companies like Uber, Postmates, Airbnb, and the like. Basically on-demand companies. Then, since you are early stage, that means you are looking for a Seed round, typically between $250,000 and $500,000, but sometimes less or more. Some investors don't invest less than $1 million or even less than $10 million; those are later stage companies, and they are looking for more traction and revenue. Others, usually Angels, will only invest small amounts. Anywhere between $10,000 and $100,000, sometimes more. You can always raise a small amount from friends and family too. A friends and family round is usually the same amount as an Angel would invest. This is typically not considered a Seed round either, it is a Pre-Seed round. For example, with Instamour, we first raised a friends and family round before we went out to try and raise a Seed round.

I soon found out that here in Philadelphia it is very difficult to raise a Seed round. But in other cities you may be able to raise $100,000-$500,000 very easily....places like Boston, New York, and Silicon Valley. Again, it really all depends on your 4 T's. In this area (the Delaware Valley), without revenue you are pretty much dead in the water. There are very few exceptions. If you have a civic, education, or healthcare startup that doesn't earn revenue, but helps the greater good, you might still have a favorable chance of raising money. Then there are VC's (Venture Capitalists). These are the big guys. They invest in the millions, and it's usually a group of VC's that all put money into the fund. Then the fund makes investments in companies.

So you want to focus on your industry, and your stage. Once you find these investment companies, then you have to go through the process that I just explained: Forming a relationship, having a warm introduction from somebody else, and having your 4 Ts in place so that you are ready. Also, make sure you have all potential investor questions answered ahead of time so that you don't mess up your first opportunity. Your first opportunity talking to an investor is usually your only opportunity. If you don't impress them, or even worse, you turn them off, you won't get a second chance. They will always remember that.

No matter what type of investor you seek or accept money from, you need to know the SEC (Securities and Exchange Commission) rules and regulations. Technically, you are only allowed to accept an investment from an accredited investor. This means you are not allowed to take money from your neighbor or your dentist. In the United States, to be considered an accredited investor, you must have at least one million dollars in the bank (not including the value of your home), or have income of at least $200,000 each year for the last two years (or $300,000 combined income if married) and have the expectation to make that same amount this year as well. So you might be asking yourself, how is it possible to raise a friends and family round from your friends and family, who (most likely) are not accredited investors? That's the most common question I get when it comes to investments. The simple answer is, that although you are technically only allowed to raise money from accredited investors, you are in fact allowed to raise money from your friends and family on a non-public level, and in a very careful way. Since this is not an institutional round of financing, you can't raise this round the way you normally would.

Legal documentation is important here, but you really don't need a lawyer to do this. What you need to do is write a proposal (or a prospectus) to your friends and family, explaining to them what kind of percentage equity in your company they will get in exchange for their money. You also have to fully disclose the plans of your company, what you will do with the money, and the risks associated with investing this money in a non-accredited, non-SEC regulated round of financing. You also have to make it very clear to them, that since they are not accredited investors, that this is purely a friends and family round to help get the company going in order to reach the level that accredited investors will be interested in.

Make sure you add to your prospectus that this is a pre-accredited investors round of funding. You also can't solicit investors publicly because that is against SEC regulation. Unless investors come to you, you can't post anything publicly saying that you are raising money. You are able to go to tech events and talk to investors, and hold private meetings, but you cannot publicly say you are raising money (even though people do it all the time). Just make sure that you are careful who you are talking to, who you raise money from, and always have documents to back you up.

Ok, so you've done all your homework, have everything in order, and actually have an investor who's interested in investing in your startup. What happens next? Well, it gets quite technical, and it always involves an attorney or attorneys. Make sure you have a good one. This can get expensive, so hopefully you have one at a local university who can help, a friend or a family member, or a lawyer who helps startups on a deferred payment basis. An investor will give you a term sheet if they are ready to invest. The term sheet is going to have a lot of legal jargon on it, and will explain how much they want to invest, at what valuation, and with any contingencies or special terms that they want. A valuation is how much your company is worth. So for example, if an investor gives your company $500,000 at a $5 million valuation, this means your company is worth $5 million pre-money, and $5.5 million post-money. It also means that the investor will be getting

10% of your company in exchange for their $500,000. If you are able to get that valuation for your Seed round, then you couldn't have done a better job in your startup.

Investors like to protect their money, and the way they do this is with "Rights, Preferences, and Restrictions." Some of the most common are anti-dilution rights (they don't lose any shares in the next funding round), the right to be first to invest in the next round, the ability to turn down other investors they don't like in the future, and the ability to purchase shares that you may want to sell before someone else buys them. There are many more special perks (or terms) they might want. Essentially, they want full control of all the decisions; they will want one or two board seats on your Board of Directors, and many other things that will make your life difficult. Believe it or not, this is pretty normal. If you are not in a good place in your company and you are raising money, the contingencies and perks get a lot worse. When you take money from an investor, you are essentially taking on a partner (or another co-founder), and you have to report to them on a regular basis so that they understand where their money is going.

This is why I tell entrepreneurs to always try to do as much as you possibly can without taking money from an investor. It is the last thing you should be doing, and you should be only doing it to scale your startup. The number one reason investors fund your startup is to earn a return on their investment. Yes, they want to help you succeed, but they want to make money; that is their goal. If you are not helping them earn revenue, then they may want to get you out of the company. Yes, even as CEO, you can be fired from your company if enough votes are in their favor. Look at what happened to Steve Jobs at Apple; he was fired from his own company in 1985. He famously came back years later, but the heartbreak he suffered from losing his company was unimaginable. Don't let that happen to you.

If you are lucky enough to be one of the 1% of startups that raises money from investors, then you should definitely celebrate. People don't realize that every time a startup raises money from investors, another couple million don't. Based on that commonly known statistic, your startup will most likely not raise any money from investors. I always tell entrepreneurs to think twice before diving into the world of tech startups. If they are doing it for the money, I tell them to stop immediately and go back to their day job. Too many entrepreneurs see the success of Facebook, Snapchat, Amazon, Uber, and all the other big companies. They don't understand that they are like Hollywood actors. How many starving actors are out there? Writers who can't get a book deal? Athletes who can't get a major sports contract? Musicians who will never get signed by a record label? The same goes for tech startups.

If you are one of the unlucky 99% who can't seem to raise money from investors, keep your chin up. There are still two things you can do to raise money: crowdfunding and accelerators. They are two completely different things, but they both work. I should know, I've successfully raised money using both methods. You probably have heard of websites such as Kickstarter.com or Indiegogo.com; they are both crowdfunding websites. The watch company Pebble recently raised $20.3 million for its' new gadget, "Time," on Kickstarter. Similar companies have funded their technology, film, video game, book, sports, or many other products or platforms on these crowdfunding sites.

When I needed to raise some money to fund to my historical documentary "The King's Highway," I exceeded my goal in 30 days[12]. Keep in mind, raising money from these crowdfunding sites is extremely difficult to do. There is a method to the madness that is crowdfunding. You have to be prepared to get the word out to your friends and family using social media, and try to get journalists to cover your story. If you can get journalists and bloggers to add the link to your campaign on an article or blog post, people will find out about it quickly. A great rule of thumb is to ask for a small amount of money in the hopes that you will reach your goal quickly so that people will see that it was successful, and then you will exceed your goal.

If you want a successful campaign, you will need to incorporate an amazing video (or trailer if you are making a movie). The video should be short, anywhere between 1 and 3 minutes. If you are selling a product, you need amazing photos or 3D models of your prototype. You also need to figure out the perks that you are giving to people. Some of the most common perks (depending on what you

---

[12]http://kickstarter.jasonsherman.org

are selling) are things like: T-shirts, posters, DVDs of your movie, a CD of your album, digital downloads, a printed book, stickers, key chains, special thanks in social media or in the credits, and things of that nature. You also need some great graphics to go along with it. People like to be stimulated visually with great photos, videos, graphics, and anything to entice them to pledge money for your campaign.

Most entrepreneurs who come to me for help with their crowdfunding campaigns think that the moment their campaign goes live is the moment that they should start to promote it. That couldn't be further from the truth. You want to put feelers out there ahead of time for potential journalists who might cover the story the day that it launches. You also want to let all your friends and family know, possibly through a Facebook event, about the day you are going to launch the campaign, so that they are ready to pledge their order. The last thing somebody wants to see when they come to a new crowdfunding page is that there are no pledges. But if it already has pledges and looks like it's gaining momentum, people are more prone to pledge money to the campaign. Additionally, crowdfunding sites look at the campaigns that are doing well, and sometimes feature them in their newsletters, and on their homepage. This will pretty much ensure success of your campaign if that happens.

The only issue with crowdfunding is that you can't really raise money for a software platform; it is mostly known to help people raise money for physical items. So if you have a physical, technological device that you want to build or mass produce, crowdfunding is the way to go. But if you are trying to raise money for a software startup, you are more than likely not going to raise the money you need on a crowdfunding site. That's what an accelerator is for. My company Instamour Inc. graduated from the StartFast Venture Accelerator in the summer of 2014 in New York[13]. It was an amazing experience, and I suggest every entrepreneur who is struggling to raise money to consider applying to various accelerators. You may have heard of something called an incubator, or a college entrepreneurial program, and things of that nature. Compared to an incubator or a college program, an accelerator is the top of the food chain when it comes to taking your startup to the next level.

So what exactly is an accelerator? It's exactly what it sounds like, it "accelerates" your growth at a rapid pace. Accelerators typically run for three months, and are run by investors or serial entrepreneurs who have succeeded in the past. The accelerator normally takes roughly 6% equity of your company in exchange for anywhere between $25,000 and upwards of $200,000 in funding. It all depends on the accelerator. Founders are usually responsible for travel and living expenses. For a New Jersey team that is accepted into a California accelerator, this can cost quite a bit. Also, some accelerators are hard to get into because they offer the

---

[13] http://startfast.jasonsherman.org

best programs in the world. Others are a little easier to get into because they are trying to get their name out there. You can find plenty of lists of accelerators on the Internet if you do a search.

Accelerators look for passionate entrepreneurs who have a disruptive idea, but they also look for the 4 Ts. The difference between an accelerator and an investor is that if you don't have the 4 Ts, but you have a solid plan of how to achieve them, you can still get accepted into one of the programs. The goal of the accelerator is for your team to achieve the 4 Ts and land a funding deal at the end of the program. The last day of the accelerator is commonly known as "demo day". That is the day when the CEO of each startup in the program pitches their platform or product in front of a roomful of hundreds of investors. If you succeeded in your goals for the program, and you interested some investors, you may get a term sheet.

Accelerators also have a network of investors who get an investment summary sent out to them from the managers of the accelerator. This way, if they weren't able to come to demo day, or if they want more information, they will receive this investment summary. Then they can reach out to you for further discussion. You are still not guaranteed funding upon completing an accelerator, but your chances are much higher. Plus, since you will be receiving some sort of funding going into the program, at least you will be able to grow your company from one stage to the next. Many startups have famously pivoted during an accelerator, whereas others just shut down because they didn't have a viable business after all.

Accelerators have an extensive application process. I've used F6S.com to apply to them in the past, which makes things much easier. I recommend that you keep all of your answers in a Google doc so that you can copy and paste them into multiple applications. If you have completed most of what I've written in this book in terms of your vision, mission, data, and everything else that we talked about, you should already have a lot of these answers. Accelerators want to know everything about your company, your team, your technology, your revenue strategy, your marketing plan, and everything else regarding your company. After all, they are investing in your company.

A warm introduction also helps when applying to an accelerator. For example, if you are trying to get into TechStars or Y Combinator and are friendly with one of their graduates, mentors, or investors - then ask them to recommend you to the accelerator via email or phone. That helps tremendously when the managing directors make a decision on who will be accepted into the next program. Many famous companies such as AirBnB, Dropbox, Reddit, and other big names graduated from an accelerator. As a matter of fact, one-third of U.S. startups that raised a Series A round (next round after Seed) in 2015 graduated from an accelerator. There is a great list of accelerators online you can check out[14]. Just be prepared to put your life on hold and move to the city where the accelerator is (unless you already live there). This is even more difficult if you are married with children. You can't take your spouse and children with you to the accelerator. Just make sure you are 100% ready for the commitment that you need to have in order to get into the program.

In the end, your goal should be to earn enough revenue each month in your startup whereas you don't need to raise money. That would be the best outcome for your company. If you can't seem to pull it off, then try raising a friends and family round to push things a bit further. Then maybe you can raise a Seed round or get into an accelerator so that you can scale your company. That's pretty much the last step for your startup: Scaling.

---

[14]http://accelerators.jasonsherman.org

Funding Stages

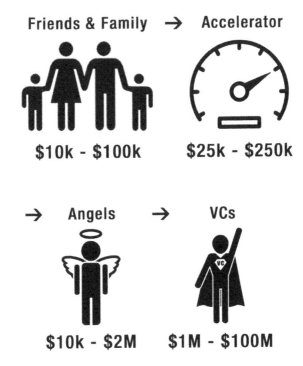

Friends & Family → Accelerator

$10k - $100k $25k - $250k

→ Angels → VCs

$10k - $2M $1M - $100M

Scaling

Since the beginning of time, humans have tried to achieve great things. Whether it was building a humongous pyramid, building a ship to cross the seas, or a spaceship to reach the moon, we have always been trying to do bigger and better things. Over the last couple of hundred years, entrepreneurs around the world have built something out of nothing. Some have achieved greatness, and others have withered away in failure. In most cases, the difference between the successes and the failures was the ability for the company to grow and scale with the demand the market asked for.

When Henry Ford first introduced his automobile the "Model T" to the world, his factory was producing these revolutionary vehicles by hand at a moderately slow rate. Once he scaled production by using the assembly line method, his production soared and he started producing the car in two and a half hours instead of 12 hours. He was able to scale his manufacturing process and change the face of the car industry (and other industries). Having the ability to do this is not always so easy. In the case of a tech startup, scaling is a little different. It usually has to do with the software platform being able to handle millions or even billions of users, like Facebook does. With a hardware product, it comes down to being able to produce mass quantities of the products, such as Apple's iPhone.

When you scale your platform, you're basically doing everything that I have outlined in this book, but in a much bigger way. Instead of getting feedback from 1,000 users, now you are getting feedback from a million users. Instead of earning revenue from 100,000 users, you may be earning revenue from 100 million users. Either way, you have to be prepared to handle the influx of that kind of bandwidth. Hosting your platform on AWS, Rackspace or another cloud-hosting solution will help you, but it won't be the entire answer. You still have to deal with security vulnerabilities, server costs, changes in software, bugs, and unforeseen circumstances that could knock your platform off the grid for 24 hours.

Before you have any issues with scaling, first you have to get to that point. So let's say that you just raised $500,000, you have roughly 400,000 users, maybe 100,000 active users, and you are earning roughly $5,000 a month in revenue. How do you take that to the next level? The first thing you want to do is identify the types of variables that will help you accelerate your business. As an example, Uber was able to identify key events in restaurants, nightlife, sports, weather, politics, and other significant events that helped dramatically boost their growth and eventually led them to become viral. By letting the data from certain market factors dictate their strategies they were able to leverage them in a big way. This is also called "Growth Hacking."

Growth hacking is a method of experimenting over various marketing channels while iterating your product so that you can figure out which of those channels is the most effective and economical way of growing your business. Usually when someone on your team is growth hacking, it is usually done in the marketing department. Believe it or not, growth hacking happens on the technology side of things too, and usually in a big way. Since you are most likely leveraging market data and statistics, as well as other platforms, you will need to integrate these into your database (or platform overall). This might sound confusing, but in fact growth hacking is the way most of the behemoth companies out there were able to scale so quickly.

Growth hacking can easily happen during the minimum viable product stage or your beta launch. You do not have to have funding in order to perform a growth hack. A famous example of this is when AirBnB allowed their early users to submit their home or apartment for rent on AirBnB and click a checkbox to also submit the same ad on Craigslist. Suddenly, thousands or even millions of people were seeing these ads on Craigslist and going to AirBnB to rent the rooms. Craigslist's lawyers sent a cease and desist letter to AirBnB which resulted in a big controversy. But the growth hack had already happened. AirBnB had already gotten millions of users and they gladly stopped posting on

Craigslist. Plus the news outlets jumped all over the story, which propelled AirBnB into the limelight.

This is the truest form of a growth hack, leveraging another platform and its user base to help grow yours quickly. Anytime you can leverage another platform, whether it be video, social, e-commerce, real estate, music, anything at all, and you can attract the users of the platform to yours while spending little to no money, is a growth hack. If you can do this, you can quickly scale your platform, and you will attract partners and investors, as well as news outlets, quickly. Then you won't have to spend as much time raising money. You will have tons of leverage if you are able to acquire millions of users with a growth hack. Plus, investors and the public will see that you were smart enough to use this technique in order to grow your company without spending a dime.

So how do you identify a growth hack in the first place? One way would be to identify platforms that are in a similar space as yours and have a lot of users. Is there a way that you can tap into their API or their network in order to attract users to your platform? Can you post your content on their platform in order to get a reciprocal sign up from users? You can also use real world events to help you find a physical connection to a growth hack. Let's say your platform lets users build a custom instrument of their choice by choosing materials, colors, graphics, and other custom pieces. Then you want to identify the specific events that trigger musicians or music lovers to either go to a musical event, or purchase an instrument. Maybe every time there is a music festival in the area, there is an uptick of instrument purchases online. Or when your local city orchestra has a special performance, more people start taking classes to learn an instrument. Either way, you want to determine what triggers a person to want to be a part of your industry, or be a customer of your product or service.

One of the great ways you can do this, especially with funding and good branding and awareness, is to partner with other companies. Local universities usually have a music program that are always willing to work with a startup. You can also talk to your local orchestras, music festivals, local bands or artists, or anyone who can help spread the word about your service. Now that you have some funding, and your name is out there, potential partners will take you more seriously. Now is when you want to approach them. The way that you do this, first and foremost, is to let them know what they will get out of the partnership. Remember, you always want to emphasize the positive in every situation. Here is an example of a letter we sent to a charity that we ended up to partnering with:

Dear [redacted name],
Instamour Inc., a new and popular tech startup company is proposing a co-marketing opportunity with the [redacted name]. With over 100 million singles in the U.S., the intent of this charitable marketing campaign is to be beneficial to both parties and build awareness to the online dating

community as well as the world of nonprofits. We are requesting to begin a "Date and Donate" campaign using our mobile app called Instamour. Every time a member purchases an upgrade on the app, they will be asked if they would like to donate $.99 cents to your charity. Instamour is a video dating platform and messaging app that allows singles to connect nationally or internationally using our video technology. If all goes well, we will establish ourselves as the first dating company to give back to a charitable organization.

We hope that your organization will find great interest in working with our company. We've long anticipated giving back to one of the most respected organizations in the U.S. and have chosen yours to be the one we would like to partner with.

You can learn more about our company here: http://instamour.com

Please let me know what the process is so that we can move forward from here.

Thank you for your time!

Kristin LaSalle
Vice President of Marketing
[number redacted]

So there are many ways that you can partner up with companies, and once you are at a certain level, they will actually want to partner with you. Companies like to reach their target market through ways that they normally wouldn't, especially when Millennials are involved. So do your best to craft a message, contact the right person at the organization or company, and make sure you make it worth their while.

While you are looking to partner up with a company, you should also be fundraising. Entrepreneurs never realize that once they have raised their first round of funding and they are scaling, they are not done raising money. Over the years, I have learned that as a CEO of a tech startup, you are constantly fundraising. As a matter of fact, as soon as you close your Seed round of say $500,000, you should immediately start changing your presentations, your numbers, and projections in order to raise a Series A round of anywhere between $1 million-$10 million.

The reason you need to do this is because as soon as you raise your Seed round, you are immediately going to begin burning through that money. This means that you need to prepare for the hiring of employees, marketing budget, development costs, server costs, and everything else that goes into your operational plan. So in order to keep the company running after your timeline, which might be one year or two years, you need to start raising the money to continue to grow the company so that you don't run out of money.

The way that you do this is to start showing the results of your first couple of months post-funding to your investors. You can use your data and projections to show what you have done in just a couple of months. This will show investors that not only are you doing what you said you would accomplish, but that you are going to succeed even further. This will of course require more resources, more time, and more money. You might notice in the news that large tech companies are constantly raising bigger and bigger rounds of financing.

Let's use Snapchat as an example. If you look at their funding rounds on popular tech company information platform Crunchbase.com you can see that Snapchat raised a large amount of money roughly every 6 - 12 months. Here is the funding chart from Crunchbase:

Snapchat Funding Rounds

$	Funding Rounds	

Announced Date	Transaction Name	Money Raised
Nov 9, 2017	Post-IPO Equity -...	$2B
May 25, 2016	Series F - Snap	$1.8B
Jul 13, 2015	Series F - Snap	—
Mar 12, 2015	Series E - Snap	$200M
Dec 31, 2014	Series D - Snap	$485M
Dec 11, 2013	Series C - Snap	$50M
Jun 23, 2013	Secondary Mark...	$20M
Jun 22, 2013	Series B - Snap	$80M
Feb 8, 2013	Series A - Snap	—
Feb 8, 2013	Series A - Snap	$13.5M
May 1, 2012	Seed Round - Snap	$485K

*Info from Crunchbase.com

This means that Snapchat CEO Evan Spiegel has been busy fundraising for the better part of the last 4 years while running the company. Fundraising constantly for your company is the way to keep growing, scaling, and achieving amazing results. It's also a way to fend off larger companies who want to buy you out or take over your company. Evan Spiegel famously turned down a $3 billion offer from Facebook. You might think that he is crazy for turning down that much money. But he was able to raise more money at almost the same valuation. Snapchat is now valued at $20 billion since they raised a $1.8 billion Series F round. So as a CEO, you have to decide if you would rather continue to raise money and grow the company, or sell the company to a larger company for a lot of money.

You also can't make the decision alone. You will typically have to host a Board of Directors meeting and company-wide meeting with people who have voting rights. This way you can host a formal vote as to whether or not you should sell the company. For example, if you hold a meeting, and you are not the majority shareholder, you could potentially lose out to a majority vote in favor of the acquisition. This means that even though you may not want to sell the company, everyone else may want to cash out. This is why one of your goals as a CEO is to try to maintain at least 51% of the voting rights of the company and/or equity in the company.

This is one of the reasons why many unicorns in the tech industry have been able to keep control of their company. They have been able to maintain their voting rights, and they continue to raise money. The question is, when should you accept an acquisition offer versus continuing to grow the company? It's a very good question, and there are many variables that go into this. Here are some of them off the top of my head:

- Do you believe the company is going to grow past the acquisition offer in value?
- Do you still believe as passionately about the company as you did when you started it?
- Are you confident that everyone in your company wants to continue working for the company?
- Do your revenue projections show that you are going to exceed the acquisition offer; if so, what is the timeframe?
- Do you have another funding round coming up that is very large and will make your valuation go past the acquisition offer?
- Do you have other ideas that you would like to start pursuing, and would like to have the funding to do so?
- Do you still want to commit all of your time and energy to this company?
- Do your cofounders and employees still want to commit all their time as well?

- Have your cofounders, employees, and Board of Directors voiced their opinions that they would like to cash out?
- What do your family and friends think?
- What does your gut say?
- If you keep the company, what are your future goals?
- Will you be able to execute those goals better than the potential acquirer?
- Do you feel comfortable with the path the potential acquirer will take with your company if they buy it?

These and other questions should be answered before you even think of accepting an offer from a large company. Look at Facebook for example. They have acquired Instagram, WhatsApp, and other companies for billions of dollars. Do you feel as though they have stayed true to the core value that those startups provided to their users? If so, then the founders of those companies made a great decision, and became very wealthy in the process. Being acquired by a larger company in some ways is the dream of every founder. Sure you can continue to grow the company, earn revenue, and raise rounds of funding to continue. Eventually you might even hold an IPO (Initial Public Offering) like LinkedIn did in 2011. Their IPO valued them at $4.25 billion out of the gate. This worked out well for them, and then in June of 2016, Microsoft acquired LinkedIn for $26.2 billion. So as you can see, you can still be acquired later on, even if you decide to pass up on other offers. It's not a one-time decision. You might be offered buyouts from several companies over the course of a couple of years. Choosing the right acquirer and price is up to you.

Just remember, whoever buys your company will be continuing your legacy long after you sell it. Also, when your company is acquired, you are typically offered a salary to continue on the staff as the transition period takes place. This is usually anywhere between one to four years, and the salary is pretty big. Let's say Google buys your company. They may ask you and your cofounders, and maybe your entire engineering team, to work for Google. Once your contract expires, you are free to do whatever you want, and with a huge bank account to boot. This means a couple of things. First, investors will want to fund whatever it is you are building next because of your exit. An exit is just another way of saying you had a successful and lucrative acquisition. This means that with your next startup, not only will you know exactly what to do because you already did it, but now you won't have to worry about fundraising as much, and will be able to just focus on building your product. You can even forget about fundraising altogether if you wish. Suppose you sold your last platform for $200 million; then you are free to invest $1 million of your own money into your new company to hire people and get things built quickly, and then spend another $1 million to market said platform. Who knows, maybe you will have another exit without taking in any investor dollars, and you will keep the entire company for yourself, your cofounders, and your employees!

Final Thoughts

Now that you understand the fundamentals of running a tech startup, you may be wondering how this can help you start another type of business. The truth is, as I help business owners in general, and not just tech entrepreneurs, I find that a lot of these basic principles work in other businesses as well. For example, somebody who wants to open a physical storefront to sell their organic dog treats will definitely want to apply most of these principles before actually opening the store. Let's say you are willing to invest $50,000 into a storefront, machinery to make the treats, order an inventory of accessories, staff, furniture, licenses and permits, signage, and everything you need to open a storefront. You have a grand opening, and business is pretty good in the beginning; but it starts to trail off, and you find yourself spending more and more money on marketing. You also see that the Internet is competing with you, because people are buying their treats online. Plus you have the big box pet stores that you are competing with as well. The next thing you know you are basically breaking even every month and it has made you miserable. So you decide that it's best to close the store down. Now you are back to reality, and you have to find a job.

Now, let's say that instead of doing it this way, you used a lot of the methods in this book. For example, did you ask yourself any of these questions before opening the store:

- How do you know customers like your dog treats as much as you think they do?
- Will your customers also purchase accessories when purchasing treats?
- Could you have made the treats out of your home, and sold the treats online instead?
- Did you send out a survey to people to ask which flavors they liked the most, which ingredients they prefer, which accessories they would want to purchase the most?
- Did you take your products to local pet conventions, dog parks, adopt-a-pet days, and other places where dog owners hang out to see what they thought of your product?
- Did you build a landing page, a blog, social media accounts, create a video, post contests, and really blast the Internet to see if people wanted to buy your products?

I can literally go on and on. Entrepreneurs need to realize that you don't have to go "all in" when it comes to starting a business. I recently met with a friend who said they wanted to quit their job and buy a franchise. When I asked how much the franchise was, they replied $30,000. I had never heard of this particular franchise. I asked if there was any data that supported how much money they were going to make in their first year in business. I also asked when they would earn their initial $30,000 back. She didn't really have the answers and said she would find out more during her first training period. I asked why they didn't want to try to start this or some other business on their own with little money upfront. The answer was, "Because this business is already running, and I won't have to do a lot of work to get things moving."

There are two main reasons people have given me as to why they are afraid to start a new business. One is because they are too busy with their job and their family. The other is because they are afraid to put in the money and hard work only to fail. If you have a full-time job, and are married with kids, I admit it is very difficult to start a new business. Even so, there is no reason why you can't spend just 30 minutes a day on a new business. You can absolutely grow your business slowly to see what can come out of it. Many successful entrepreneurs over the years have done this. It's just like writing this book. I spent maybe one hour every day writing it, and after six weeks I had completed the first version of the book. I didn't sit here and spend eight hours a day writing it; I spent an hour here and there when I had time. Sure, some days I was able to commit up to four hours writing, but that wasn't the norm. That's how you should treat a new business if you are married with kids, or if you have a full-time job.

So stop worrying about the money, the time, and the success of your new business. Instead think about the journey, the learning experience, and how much fun it will be to work on something other than your job. The journey is probably the most important part of starting a new company. As Ralph Waldo Emerson once said, *"Life is a journey, not a destination."* Once you treat your company as a daily joy, instead of looking toward the ultimate destination, you will learn to love the process that much more. Enjoying what you do is one of the most powerful things you can do in your life. Being a serial entrepreneur since 2005, I've been fortunate enough to enjoy every second of what I do for a living. As Confucius once said:

Choose a job you love, and you will never have to work a day in your life.

That saying is so true, because I feel like I haven't been working since my last corporate job in 2005. Instead I feel like I've been enjoying life while creating companies that have brought me (and other people) much joy. I have spoken with so many people who are tired of the monotony of their full-time, corporate job. They read the news and see all the success stories. They tell me, "Wow, look at all these entrepreneurs who are living the life." Of course, they don't understand how difficult it is to run a company; all they see the glitz and glamour. The trick is to find something that you truly love about this world. Maybe you like animals. So why not work at an animal shelter. Sure, you might not make as much money as your finance job, but you will come home satisfied and happy knowing that you helped save some animals.

I recently spoke to a friend who works for a large law firm. He told me that he really couldn't take the stress of his job anymore and was just plain miserable. One day, a friend of his offered him a job to work as a telephone line installation specialist at the U.S. Virgin Islands. The job offered half of the pay that he was earning now, but a lot of his expenses would be included. The company would pay for his training, a small villa to live in, and relocation expenses. He ended up taking the job. I recently spoke to him, and now he says that he is "on a permanent vacation." He works on beautiful beaches out in the sun installing telephone lines, and only has to work a couple of hours a day. The rest of the time he spends scuba diving, jet skiing, soaking up the sun, enjoying the nightlife, and hanging out with his new friends on the island. He told me something that I've always thought to be true, "Money isn't everything. Sure it's nice to have, but my freedom and happiness is much more valuable."

That's just it, by finding something that you love, your time will be well spent. This means that you won't regret what you did with your time later in life. You will be happy with the choices that you made. When someone tells me they are unhappy with their job, I tell them that it's never too late to learn a new skill or start a new career.

They always roll their eyes, sigh, and say that they don't have the time to learn a new skill, and it's too late. Telling me that it's too late to learn something new or change your profession is one of the most ridiculous things I've ever heard. For the past 11 years I have researched, learned, and become an expert in several industries. Every time I was interested in a new topic, I would dive deep into it. Sometimes it would turn into a business, and sometimes it would just help me understand the world better. Either way, I always kept one thing in mind:

It's never too late to learn something new and change your path.

I could list tons of celebrities, inventors and entrepreneurs who didn't succeed in a global way until their late 30s, 40s, 50s, and even 60s. Instead, I will say this: the only time it is too late to do something new is when you are dead and buried. So while you are alive, why not maximize the value in your life by learning new things. By trying new things regularly, you will never give up being an entrepreneur. When mentors, gurus, investors and famous people say to never give up, it's the truth. Don't worry so much about having to close down a company, or not pursuing an idea that you originally thought was good. Just don't give up on learning, building, and being a part of something bigger than yourself. If you do end up having to close a company down, it doesn't mean you are giving up.

It means that you will take the lessons you learned and will apply them to something new without the previous mistakes.

As Nicola Tesla once said, *"Our virtues and our feelings are inseparable, like force and matter. When they separate, man is no more."*

The key is to try and enjoy every second of the journey. If you are always thinking about the destination, you won't see the intricacies and details that go into arriving there. Details are part of the learning process that you need in order to have a happy outcome. I've seen countless entrepreneurs raise large amounts of money and always talked about the destination. But their journey was very short and miserable because of the quick failure. When you first start your company, everything has to be laid out so that you can see where you are going and how you will get there. This will make your journey much more fluid.

You can't let mistakes and errors get you down. You have to just breathe, and realize that everything will be OK. Whatever you put into a project is exactly what you will get out of it. As you know, your energy travels throughout the universe, and it comes back to you tenfold. Always stay positive, be passionate, and always encourage your team.

"By prevailing over all obstacles and distractions, one may unfailingly arrive at his chosen goal or destination." - **Christopher Columbus**

A cool startup hack I recommend is to portray a status that is bigger than it is. I've done this various times. When I was a sophomore in college (mid 90s) I started RaveGear.com as a well-known DJ/producer. Hundreds of DJs would send in their demo tapes because they thought we were a large company. The website was one of the first to sell rave merchandise, and we had a thriving message board along with solid music sales. I did have over 1,000 promoters throughout the United States, and a DJ roster of 10 at the time, so it seemed like I was big. But the truth was that I was just a guy in a house running a million dollar EDM (rave) company. Yes, I had a big company, but it seemed bigger than it was from the outside.

"Fake it till you make it," they say. Well I faked it and I made it. So why not try it out. If you are always positive when you speak to people about what you do, they may find you are worth investing in, whether it be time or money. Just make sure you know what you are talking about. Your online presence also matters in a big way. With Instamour for example, I was fortunate enough to have some great press and media early on during the company's growth in 2014. This made our company look huge, and we were contacted by tons of companies that wanted to help us monetize, and entrepreneurs who wanted to work for us.

Just make sure that you can live up to the hype you are delivering. I've met plenty of entrepreneurs who could talk a big game, but couldn't deliver. That's dangerous in the realm of tech startups. Once you burn through all your funding without a shiny new product, investors will rarely continue to invest in you. Word spreads through the investor community, and almost immediately you will have no interest (or funding). I have seen rare exceptions, with a resulting second failure. It still shocks me to this day. This is why pivoting is so powerful.

If you are lucky enough to have funding, a great team, and everything I listed in this book, then that means you're smart enough to pivot if you need to. When you run a business of any kind, instead of looking at a pivot as a crutch, you should look at it as an evolution of your business. The world is changing every day. Things are getting faster and they are getting easier. Let's face it, we are living in the future already. With innovations such as self-driving cars, the Internet, smartphones, virtual reality, drones, and artificial intelligence, we are living in a science-fiction movie. So in order to stay relevant in such an evolving (and saturated) world of technology, sometimes you need to pivot in order to leverage your assets to create a new opportunity.

It might be just a small pivot, nothing major. One small tweak into a different market or different trajectory could make a million dollar difference. Keep in mind that you should always be using your data to drive your decisions. So if the majority of e-commerce sales on your platform are coming from South America, why is that exactly? When it comes to a pivot, you should always be asking yourself some key questions. Here are some of them:

- What product(s) are the most popular in South America?
- What is the age range of the people buying them?
- Are there any data trends that you can capitalize on?
- What is your CPA, CPI, CPC (and other metrics) - and how do they differ with your other locations and demographics?
- What are your revenue projections within this data set?

Finding out the answers to these and other questions could prove to be valuable. You might find out that your platform could earn a substantial amount of revenue in South America and you may tweak your startup to reflect that. You could even build a vertical strictly for that market, branding and all. Let's say that you noticed your users were watching the video ads you integrated on your platform more in South America than they were in Europe, Asia or North America. Your data also told you that those same users weren't really making any purchases. So you dig into your analytics to find out that the most common sites they frequently visited were sports sites. So maybe you could then build a platform that focused on sports videos, forums, message boards, merchandise, etc. Then you could focus on this obvious niche market and really start to scale fast. I could give you many examples, but only you can decide what to do in the end. When it comes to pivoting, always think outside the box, research market trends, look for a niche, and create a new space if you can. Don't sit still. Always move forward, study data, and in the process, you will be breathing new life into your startup.

Your cofounders and team will appreciate this mode of working. The last thing your team wants to feel is stuck in their job without any chance of new challenges or potential growth. They could have just stayed at their last corporate job instead of joining your startup if they wanted to do that. Implementing fresh ideas goes hand in hand with leading a healthy lifestyle as well. Every time you go to the gym, ride your bike, eat a salad, or play a sport, you reinvigorate your body. Well, the same goes for your startup. Keep it fresh and healthy. I personally take a certain amount of breaks every day. There are many studies that state entrepreneurs work 16 hours a day, 7 days a week. I need to clarify something. While I may work a lot of hours, it's not consecutive. Here's an example of a typical workday for me:

7:30 AM – 8 AM: Wake up, walk my dog Wolfy.

8:15 AM: Breakfast / coffee / stretch.

9 AM: Work at my standing desk.

10:30 AM: Ride my bicycle to the gym for a workout (or exercise at home).

12 PM: Make a smoothie for lunch and get back to my standing desk for work. Sit when I get tired.

2 PM: Take Wolfy to the park for my coffee break.

2:30PM: Come up with brilliant ideas.

3 PM: Back to my desk to do more work.

6 PM: Take a shower, make dinner, call it a day.

But here is the difference between a regular job and an entrepreneur. Between 7PM and 11PM while I am not technically "working," I might still be answering emails, taking phone calls, hosting video conferences, going to events, jotting down ideas, researching, reading, teaching, or anything and everything associated with my companies. This doesn't mean that it is happening from 7PM to 11PM, and it also doesn't mean that it's happening every day. There are some nights where you are literally able to just take off. Whereas other nights, things pop up and you have to take care of them. It might only be a few minutes here and there throughout those hours. But it means that you do not have to be sitting (or standing) at your desk, since you have this amazing invention called a smartphone.

My point is that you need to take a decent amount of breaks. You also need to take days off. So if you work really hard for a couple of days, why not take off on a Thursday or a Friday, or both? I do it all the time. As an entrepreneur, I don't have the luxury of paid two-week vacations, so I take mini-vacations on a regular basis. I also have taken my employees on these mini-vacations, and I regularly have invited my cofounders to getaways. By involving your team and your cofounders on fun activities, or getaways, you will keep everyone energized and happy. At least once a year I do take a one or two week vacation somewhere in the world; in the winter when it's cold where I live I usually go to a place where it is warm. I recommend you do the same.

Not only should you develop an extremely flexible work/life balance, but you need to give credit where it is due, on a regular basis. And you need to delegate. Years ago, one of my mentors told me to allow other people to do important work for one of my businesses. When I did that, I started to see the business grow in a way that I was never able to do alone. It's no secret that if you have other smart people working with you, the results will be twofold or threefold depending on how many people you have on your team. One of the things I like to do to show my appreciation is praise my team or cofounders when they do a good job. I do this on a regular basis. Keeping everyone's spirit high by letting them know that you appreciate their hard work helps keep the overall mood of your company positive.

Some of you might have heard about how Steve Jobs was considered a tyrant at Apple. Many employees would complain about how mean he was. He would regularly scream at employees in meetings, fire people on the spot, and was not very friendly at work. I suggest you do the opposite. Praise people in meetings, fire them privately (if you have to), and be as nice to your coworkers and cofounders as you would be to your family members. The great thing about doing this is that your employees and cofounders will speak highly of you in public, with friends and family, other startups, and investors. This means you won't have to talk about yourself, which is a good thing.

I've never really liked an entrepreneur who brags about the things they have done, or how great their life is, or their startup. Actions speak louder than words. The most successful entrepreneurs I've ever met have been the ones who have not bragged about what they have done. Instead they have just shown me their work, their ideas, or their results. From there I can determine whether or not they have been successful. Even when you are successful, or when you reach a big milestone, you have to always remember to stay humble.

I'm not saying that you can't celebrate your successes, or enjoy the fruits of your labor with your cofounders or team. I'm just saying don't go bragging around town that your startup is the best one out there. Let's say your startup just reached 1 million users and you are killing it. That's great, so host a celebration with your friends, family, and cofounders. Then, keep your head down and continue to plug away, because your journey has not ended yet. I've noticed that companies, entrepreneurs, interns, college students, and just everyday people want to be involved with a company that has the perception of being a success.

If you are the one pushing that perception, then it's not as valid as it is if the market is saying that it's a success. A good example of this would be if a singer named Jill started singing on the streets of New York, in the subway, bus stops, and in front of restaurants. She would post videos online and share them with her friends, family, and her social media followers. She keeps telling everyone that she's going to be the next big thing, bigger than Taylor Swift. She may or may not be a good singer, although that doesn't really matter. What matters is what people think. If she keeps telling everyone she's going to be the best, they're probably just going to brush her off as "just another singer" who doesn't realize how hard it is to make it big and get a record deal.

If instead of focusing on how great she is, and how big she's going to get, if she focused on training her voice, taking voice lessons, emulating famous singers by watching their videos, learning the theory behind music, and truly becoming an expert in the field of music, then she might have a chance. If she did all that, and then started to go out to sing again, enter competitions, even try out for TV shows, who knows, maybe the public will embrace her. If she stays humble, and true to her craft, learning every aspect of singing, and lets the public decide whether or not she is the next big thing, then she will most likely succeed.

She may not get a record deal, but maybe she'll be hired by a company to be a singer for weddings, or cruises, or maybe even on Broadway. Success comes in many forms; whether or not she lands a multimillion dollar record deal doesn't necessarily mean success. Getting paid to sing is her ultimate goal. So she should be focusing on everything she can do to reach that goal. Telling people she's going to make it isn't going to help, but working her butt off day and night to reach that goal is how she's going to make it. So remember, don't brag, and stay as humble as possible.

One of the ways you can learn how to be successful is to listen to people who have succeeded. Listening is one of the most powerful things you can do in life. Everyone likes to talk about themselves, so listen to what they have to say. It took me a long time to learn this. I thought I had all the answers. I was wrong. I'm saving you time by telling you to:

Listen, listen, and listen.

When you are at a networking event, listen to people when they talk to you. When you are in a meeting with investors, listen to what they have to say. Don't interrupt them. Over time I learned a neat little trick. When you are listening to somebody, put your finger over your mouth as if you are resting your hand. Just put one finger over your lips to remind yourself to listen. This way it seems like you are really paying attention, but also it'll stop you from interrupting someone. It sounds silly, but it works.

When you ask for advice, feedback, or suggestions for one of your companies, don't keep interrupting somebody to tell them that you've already done those things, or that you've already tried those things. Instead, relax and listen to everything the person has to say, no matter how trivial it may seem. If you listen, you may find out what the person has to say is actually pretty smart or important. You just have to let them get it out. Interrupting them may cause them to lose their train of thought. Also, they may find it to be rude, and they may not want to continue to tell you all of their valuable feedback.

Also, by listening you will see the types of questions people ask you, and the way they talk to you. This helps you learn how to talk to people. Especially in the tech industry, there are a lot of buzz words people use, and the vocabulary is pretty specific. So by listening to people talk, you can learn those words. This helps you fit it quickly. When you listen to people, they feel as though you care about what they are saying, which makes them feel more important. They will be more inclined to help you in the future if you just thank them for all of the things they just told you. You may actually get some valuable feedback, just by listening to somebody. Then, when you ask a question, listen to what they have to say. Ask another question, and listen to what they have to say. Keep your questions short, and keep your replies short. Focus on listening to the person that you are talking to.

I love Dale Carnegie's book *"How to Win Friends and Influence People"*. There are some great bits of advice in there. Two that I will tell you about are:

Become genuinely interested in other people. You can make more friends in two months by being interested in them, than in two years by making them interested in you.

Be a good listener. Encourage others to talk about themselves. The easiest way to become a good conversationalist is to become a good listener. To be a good listener, you must actually care about what people have to say. Many times people don't want an entertaining conversation partner; they just want someone who will listen to them.

So not only is listening a way to gain new friends, but it also helps you learn how to become better at speaking. One of the best things I learned from listening to people over the years is the types of things that I excel at, and places where I have a weakness. One of the things that people have told me time and time again, is that my organization and prioritization skills are superb. I realized that when working with new entrepreneurs or companies, they usually lack organization and are not effectively prioritizing their tasks. For every company that I have started, you will find a fully organized set of documents and folders, and you will always be able to find a particular document within seconds. You will find priority lists, task lists, mission statements, plans of action, operational plans, and any other major priorities listed out. This holds you accountable for every document or task.

This isn't just for your company, it is for your life also. Organizing your documents, your office, your company priorities, and anything associated with your company or your life, should be second nature to you. If you have everything organized and you have your priorities spelled out, then you will always have a direct path to success. If you just start working and doing things on the fly, and patching holes whenever you hit a wall, you will be digging yourself into a deep, dark hole. I've had to help entrepreneurs climb out of that hole many times, and restructure, reorganize, and prioritize their company and even their lives.

One of the best ways you can do this is to spend some time writing out a list of every document you need, and which department the document is in. You should also write up a document listing the tasks you need to do for your company, as well as which department they are in. Here are examples of these documents, in no particular order of importance (including but not limited to):

Corporate:

- Mission statement
- Vision for the future
- Revenue goals
- Technology milestones
- Marketing milestones
- Company culture
- Employee onboarding process
- Job titles and roles
- Work schedule
- Investor contact spreadsheet
- Corporate contact directory
- Slack channel for communication
- Board meeting schedule
- Employee meeting schedule
- Scrum meeting schedule
- Company architecture
- Office logistics, equipment & supplies
- Corporate documentation repository
- Investor deck
- Corporate online presence

Legal & Investors:

- Executive summary
- Operational agreement
- Non-Disclosure agreement
- CAP table
- Investment summary
- PowerPoint presentation
- Business plan
- Advisory board agreement
- Board of directors agreement
- Board of directors minutes checklist
- Articles of incorporation
- Letter to shareholders
- Stock purchase agreement
- Common stock certificate
- Nonqualified stock option agreement
- Stock option exercise agreement
- Consultant confidentiality and inventions assignment agreement
- Independent contractor agreement
- IP assignment agreement

Marketing & Branding:

- Company logo
- App icons
- Slogans
- Campaign ideas
- Online survey
- Mailchimp account and integrations
- Landing page with email sign-up
- Company website
- Blog setup and content distribution
- Graphic image repository
- Company video
- App Demo video
- Popular industry keyword spreadsheet
- Target market demographics
- Social media accounts
- Social media management
- Email templates
- Newsletter designs
- Press release template
- Ambassador program documentation
- Brochure or flyer
- College intern manual
- On-boarding process documentation
- Contests & Giveaways
- Promotional swag

- Celebrity tie-ins

Technology & Development:

- Technical workflow document
- Visual workflow maps
- Overall architecture document
- Sliced PNG images for mobile
- Database integration
- Front facing website
- API integrations
- Scalable hosting service
- Google analytics (or other analytics)
- Private Github account
- Security precautions
- Color style guide
- Icon style guide
- Font style guide

Again, these are just some examples and definitely are not all of the items that might belong on your list. For example, most of this may not even apply to you if your company revolves around a new product you are selling. But for the most part, the items on these lists have been commonly used in the startups I worked with or ran. The goal is to create a list for each department that relates to your company. This way you have actionable items that you can cross off your list when you tackle them. One great way to utilize technology to do this is to put these lists into a spreadsheet and assign them to people, or better yet use Trello.com and assign employees to each task. Believe it or not, I have done the same thing for my personal life, and I have been able to get to the point where I am happy with every aspect of my life. Everything is incremental; you have to take things step-by-step, and day by day.

I've noticed that people struggle to reach a certain lifestyle they want. It's not that they are living beyond their means; it's that the world has been rapidly advancing in terms of cost, but the overall work industries have not increased salaries. One way that I have counteracted this is by doing the opposite: I've minimized my expenses. People think that earning a large income will equal success. That may be true, but if you have tons of bills, then that large amount of money will easily be sucked up by those bills. If you want to be a successful, full-time entrepreneur, then you have to do everything you can to keep your expenses as minimal as possible.

You can do this in various different ways. Some of these ways might seem trivial, but they add up in the long run. For example, instead of buying coffee at a store every day, I make my own coffee. Since I drink 2 cups a day, that's a savings of $3,650 each year if I were to go to Starbucks, or $1,825 if I were to go to Dunkin' Donuts. I buy certain items in bulk, which saves time and gas money driving to the store. I don't buy cleaning supplies; instead I buy big bottles of white vinegar and mix it with water into spray bottles. Not only am I avoiding harsh chemicals, but I am saving money. I don't lease my car, I bought it outright so I own it. I don't rent my house, I bought it, so I own it. This saves money because instead of wasting money on rent, I am slowly owning more and more of my house. Eventually I won't owe anything on my house and I will have a big asset. Also in the past, I had programmers build apps with me while living in my house and paying rent. This has offset my mortgage for years. I don't have any credit card debt either, and that's important.

I ride my bicycle to and from the gym if the weather permits; this not only gives me more exercise, but it saves gas money and the time that I would've had to warm up at the gym. In total I am saving about $7,800 a year (minus bad weather). Plus I'm saving roughly $260 in gas per year since I don't use my car those days. Believe me when I tell you, every dollar adds up.

I don't take my dog to the groomer. Which reminds me, get a dog. They are great stress relievers, and will give you a reason to take a break and go for a walk. If you are having a bad day, just go pet your dog, and they will give you unconditional love and cuddles. As for my dog, I cut his hair, brush his teeth, cut his nails, and give him baths at my house. That saves me $60 every time I do it myself plus that pesky travel time. That's roughly another $1,000 a year I'm saving. I don't use a ton of paper products. Instead I use anything that I can wash and use again. Not only is it better for the environment, but it saves money. The same goes for food; I buy groceries every couple of days, nice and fresh, and I cook lunch and dinner regularly, which saves money instead of going out all the time. Not only is it healthier, but it saves money.

I can go on and on, but in the end, you just have to minimize your expenses so that instead of having to earn a super large income, instead you can earn an average income and still live like a wealthy person. You can still have all the gadgets and toys that you want, take vacations, buy clothes, go to the movies, go out to dinner with your friends, catch a show on Broadway, or any other thing that you want to do. You will be able to spend money on things that you need or want if you are saving in other ways. By minimizing your expenses, you won't have the pressure of a mountain of bills holding you back from bootstrapping your startup. Not only that, but you won't have to seek funding from investors so soon. The startups I was a part of that failed were because my cofounders couldn't keep working for equity. They needed to pay their bills, and we weren't able to raise additional funding in time. So we had to close down the companies and they had to go find jobs. I was the only one that was always able to continue without worrying so much about getting a job. Granted, I own a technology consulting company, and have other sources of income. Still, I wasn't pressured to "get a job" to "pay the bills," while my cofounders were.

One of the perks of not having your financial situation pressure you into making decisions you wouldn't normally make is the ability to help people around you. I've been fortunate enough to provide my consulting services or volunteer as a mentor to entrepreneurs and startups for the better part of a decade. High school and college students are the entrepreneurs who need the most help. Since I don't worry about my financial situation, I've been able to help the students, which in turn helps me.

You would be surprised what you can learn from teaching others. Everyone has their own methods, styles, tools, and workflow. By teaching and mentoring others, you will potentially find new ways of doing things. Not only does it feel really good to help someone who truly needs it, but if you become a part of a company, and you earn equity in the process, you could potentially have a big success on your hands. You don't have to always be the CEO of every startup. As a matter of fact, it is extremely healthy and intelligent for you to just be a part of a startup and help it grow. By seeing how others run their company, you could also learn a bit about how to run your next one.

This works the other way as well. By working with startups, you can see how they fail, and how they make mistakes, so that you can avoid making them in the future. One of the things that you would rarely think about when it comes to helping people, although it is very important, is that you are exercising your brain. When going through the steps of building a startup from scratch, you are using your brain as the muscle it was meant to be. Plus, since you have already done it before, everything will be much easier for you the second or third time around. You'll start to see that my methodologies are useful not just in a tech startup, but in a business of any kind, your health, your life, or your family and friendships.

Working with entrepreneurs in a startup is like working with a family. You are all closely related in some way, and you all have a common goal. You start to feel like a team, like brothers and sisters, mothers and fathers, or close friends. If you don't have close family or friends, then being in a startup is the next best thing. So by helping other people, you might in fact find yourself in a familial situation. In the case of being a mentor, think of it as being the coach of an NBA basketball team. The players need guidance, tactics, support, and motivation. Nothing feels better than winning a championship, but the journey to get there is what you'll remember for years to come.

Part of this journey entails research and learning. One of the first things I tell an entrepreneur who says they want to build a mobile app, website, or physical product, is that they need to research and learn everything they can about the market they are about to enter. In my opinion, research is one of the most important pieces of a startup. I can't tell you how many times an entrepreneur pitches their idea to me, only for me to find the exact same idea already in the marketplace. Then they tell me that their idea is different, and that they are going to "crush the market." Then I ask them to show me examples of their differentiation, and how they plan to "crush the market." Usually, their plan is to just build some extremely difficult (with every bell and whistle) product that they think people will want. But they hardly ever have any concrete data to back up their theory. A little research goes a long way.

Doctors don't perform brain surgery right off the bat. They need to research and learn everything to do with the medical field for years before they even touch a scalpel. Before you build anything or spend your valuable time and money, make sure you research the market entirely. For example, let's say you want to build a new platform that helps you grow plants. Then you should go to Google and type in: 'plant growing apps'. Read articles on TechCrunch, Mashable, Cnet, Wired, HuffPost, and even read forums on Reddit. Research plant blogs, read articles from certain journalists, and even pick up a horticulture magazine or newspaper. You want to wrap your head around the entire plant industry, where it is headed, what technologies have been invented, what the yearly revenue is, and many other factors.

For example, from my research I have found out that the plant industry is growing in a different way than expected. More indoor vertical farms are popping up, rather than traditional outdoor soil farming. Indoor vertical farms use less energy, no soil, and are able to grow higher yields in less space than outdoor farming. This is disrupting agriculture. So if you plan on building an app to help you with this new disruption, you need to know everything about it. This could mean visiting an indoor farm, or even an outdoor farm. Find out what the pain points are in the industry from people who buy plants, whether consumers, restaurants, or grocers. Essentially you need to know everything about the plant market. This will take time, and patience.

While you are researching and learning about your space, over time you are actually becoming an expert in the field of entrepreneurship. By becoming an expert, you are adhering to the 10,000 hour rule, which isn't the end all be all, but it definitely holds some clout. Most famous people throughout history became an expert through practice, making mistakes, and the ability to adapt to any situation.

Sir Richard Branson is a great example of this. He started in the record business with Virgin Music, and now the Virgin Group owns over 400 companies and they are even sending people to space. He became an expert in building companies and he adapted to various industries. If you add up the hours, 10,000 of them equal roughly 3 years of your time. I've become an expert in the realm of technology, videography, music, writing, art, and other things that I have dedicated my life to. Not only does this add credibility to your background when investors are checking you out, but it allows you to thrive in various different ways. You can either be a jack of all trades and a master of none, or a jack of few trades and a master of some. That is much more powerful.

I've seen entrepreneurs with a PhD in a particular field acquire funding much more easily for the field in which they have a PhD. For example, rarely does a PhD in history help you get funding for a startup in the music industry, or a Master of Economics help you get funding for a startup in the fashion industry. It helps when you are an expert in the field of which you are building your startup. If you are not, then it's a good idea for you to find other experts who will complement your skills. Maybe you are building a new heart rate monitor for your wrist, but you have a background in engineering. So you might need someone who has a medical background to understand the nuances of the heart rate. You also might need someone who is an expert in building molds or putting together electronic parts. You would be the one who can code the app and build the technology infrastructure, but your other experts will back you up on the other pieces.

Over time you may find that you became an expert (by chance) and built an app or product out of need. This has happened to me several times. While you are working in a certain industry you may come across a pain point; something that makes your daily work more of a struggle. You would have never found this pain point if you weren't learning and becoming an expert in that field. Part of becoming an expert is practice, practice, practice. By practicing methodologies, implementing experiments, and learning everything you need to know about a particular industry, you are actually practicing to become an expert in something. It is imperative that you feel comfortable in the industry that you chose to become an expert in. As I said before, you need to commit at least three years (or 10,000 hours) in something to become an expert. As the saying goes: *"Practice makes perfect."* I always say, *"Practice makes you an expert."*

Make sure you are prepared to commit your time and your life to this particular company, idea, or topic. You have to mentally prepare yourself. If not, you will want to give up as soon as you hit a roadblock. There was a point in my life where I hit a roadblock, and I felt stuck in the particular industry that I was in. I was ready to throw in the towel when I met someone who changed my life forever. He was my first real mentor. Even though he wasn't a substantial part of my life, he was a seasoned entrepreneur who had been through it all. He saw my roadblock, but he also saw my intelligence, talent, and will to succeed.

He told me that I had to give up control of my work. That I had to find other people to help me do the work. He made it very clear to me that the work may not be perfect, but it will get done, and it will allow me to do other things while the work was getting done. I have to admit, this was very difficult for me to do, because up until then, I was getting everything done by myself, and it was working great. I just wasn't able to grow my business. Also, I wasn't able to get into another business because I was stuck in the current one. He didn't even really care so much about what the business was. He was looking at things on the surface. As a matter of fact, he said I would be doing great things with my life, not just the current business. He was more concerned with my personal well-being, where my head was, and how I felt about my life.

The point is, you need to find at least one mentor who has been through it all, and will help guide you on the right path. The reason I know this is true is because I have been mentoring many entrepreneurs for years now. I have been able to impart my knowledge to them as well. I've been able to transform entrepreneurs' lives, and will continue doing so for the rest of my life. If it wasn't for my original mentor, who knows, I might still be stuck in that old business.

Another part of being an expert is figuring out what pieces of the industry are most important to learn in order to become an expert. I say this because in the past I taught myself many things that I could have bypassed in order to get to the root of the value proposition in that industry. I've spent countless hours and thousands of dollars learning things or trying things that I really could have done without. But that's part of becoming an expert; learning from your mistakes and figuring out the best way to do things. The point of my book is to help you avoid that, and instead really pinpoint which pieces of your industry are the most important (or valuable) and focus on those.

Jot down a list of the results that you're looking for in becoming an expert in the industry. Based on those bullet points, figure out which methods of research will enable you to become an expert in those points. For example, let's say that you want to become an expert in filmmaking. Here's what the bullet list might look like:

- Watch movies in the genres you are interested in
- Read award-winning screenplays
- Learn the history of filmmaking (going back to the 1890s)
- Shadow other filmmakers as an intern
- Work as an intern for production houses or movie studios
- Buy a legitimate camera and learn how to use it properly
- Watch videography tutorial videos on YouTube
- Get out there and shoot some content
- Build or purchase your video editing studio
- Learn how to properly edit your video content
- Learn how to merge music with video
- Hang out with other filmmakers
- Go to local film festivals to see what local filmmakers have been producing

Now that you have your bullet list, your goal is to figure out the best methods to perform these tasks. Luckily for you, most of these resources will be found on the Internet. The bullet list I wrote above is something that I actually started roughly 10 years ago. Three years into my research, I wrote, produced, and directed my first feature film[15] which won the audience choice award at a film festival in 2011, and is currently distributed worldwide. So I know for a fact that it takes roughly 3 years to become an expert in something.

Then, in July of 2016 I completed my second film, a historical documentary about Philadelphia[16]. It won the "Best Feature Documentary" award at the 2016 FirstGlance film festival, had its' movie premiere at Philadelphia's number one venue, the Kimmel Center for the Performing Arts in December of 2016, played on WHYY/PBS for the entire 2017 TV season, and is now distributed globally by Indie Rights, a Los Angeles based distributor. The production quality is miles ahead, the story is compelling, and I have attracted politicians, organizations, historians, as well as thousands of residents and community members on social media and in local screenings.

The reason I'm telling you about my film projects is because I want you to know that you too can do this. Everything I am telling you is easily replicable if you are willing to put in the time, the energy, some money, and your passion. Every time I embarked on a new journey, a new project, or a new company, I would constantly visualize my goals. This is very important, and I hold this to be true. You probably have heard people say this before.

---

[15] http://BucksCountyMovie.com
[16] http://KingsHighwayFilm.com

Visualization is key. You really need to meditate and think about what it is you want your life to be like. If you can list the priorities that you want in your life and how you want your life to be, you can slowly reach your goals not just for your business, but your life.

Try to think back to when you were a kid, when you would think about being a superhero, or a famous athlete. You had these fantasies about what you wanted to be when you grew up. I remember playing basketball on the court with my friends when I was about 16 years old, and everybody would say, I can't wait till I'm older so I can drive, or so I can buy a house. When everyone asked me what I wanted to do, I said I just wanted to be an entrepreneur. They didn't really get it. They thought I was crazy. They would ask me, "But what do you want to do for a living?" I would reply, "I want to create awesome companies and enjoy my life." I visualized having a flexible schedule, earning an income doing what I love, and creating amazing companies.

Ever since that day, I worked toward the goal of becoming an entrepreneur. I visualized what I wanted my life to be like. I would regularly sit with my eyes closed (still do), and imagine what my life would be like if I had everything I ever wanted. Every time I would achieve one of the goals on that mental list, I would feel fulfilled in some way. As I got older, I would start to actually write out a list of what I wanted out of my life. Slowly I would start to attain each bullet point on that list. By visualizing each skill, gadget, personal goal, or business goal, I was setting expectations for myself. Visualizing your goals is also very calming. It feels good to just unwind and fantasize about what your life could be like. For the longest time, my main goal was to have freedom. Freedom to do what I wanted whenever I wanted. Freedom to set my own schedule. Freedom to be able to start companies without the worry of financial burden. Freedom to be able to help others without worrying about personal consequences of time. When I finally realized that I had achieved that freedom, I felt as though I achieved my greatest life goal.

To figure out what your greatest life goal is, whether it's to build the next big app, a life-changing gadget, becoming a recording artist, olympic athlete, filmmaker, doctor, lawyer, dog groomer, or philanthropist, visualize the list of tasks needed to achieve that ultimate goal. You will find yourself slowly reaching that goal if you dream about it, think about it, and work towards it. One day, you may find yourself living the life that you always wanted. It happened to me, so I know it can happen to you.

When you are a full-time, serial entrepreneur (like myself), typically you are working on multiple projects at a time. When building a company, as I mentioned in this book, there is a process that you have to go through, from whiteboard to launch. On a daily basis, your focus is usually devoted to each piece of this process. Each product or service has a different process. Along the way you will most likely learn some things, and those skills you will learn are very valuable. In order to keep your mind focused and sharp, you should get used to creating or coming up with new ideas every few months. This doesn't mean that you should build new companies every few months. It simply means that you should get used to the process of creating the foundation for a new idea. At the very least, jot down your new ideas on a notepad or "in the cloud" so that you don't forget them.

Not only will this keep your skills sharp, but when you do succeed in one of your ideas and potentially earn a sizable income you will have a plethora of ideas ready to take to the next level. Also, investors do invest in entrepreneurs as well as ideas. They will like the fact that you have a whole portfolio of ideas waiting to be created. Not only will you be an expert at starting a new company, but you will know the ins and outs of how to manage each aspect of the company, including the employees needed to run each department.

If one day you decide you'd like to be a consultant and help other companies succeed in various ways, you will have the skills, knowledge, and resources available to do just that. New products, platforms, tools, resources, and design specs come out every day. Companies like Google and Apple set new standards for UI/UX, so it's good to keep up with all of that incorporated into the daily routine of your startup. If you follow this advice you will always be up to date, and you always have the newest and best practices ingrained in your company. Worst case scenario, if none of your ideas ever get to a Series A funding round, or earn you enough revenue to quit your day job, you will still become an expert at building a product. Luckily in this day and age, that is a valuable skill to possess.

One more thing that I always tell my students or entrepreneurs that I mentor is to try and be an early adopter for new technologies. For example, in 2013 I was fascinated by Bitcoin and cryptocurrencies. I taught myself how to build a mining rig to mine Bitcoin and learned how to trade Bitcoin for other Altcoins. Little did I know that it would become a worldwide phenomenon years later. I used the knowledge that I gained, and investments I made to build another mining rig to mine Ethereum in 2016 and 2017. Apparently most people in the crypto space nowadays got into crypto in late 2017 (and a lot of them lost money). I thought I was late to the game in 2013, but apparently I was super early.

So I implore you to learn as much as possible, and try new things as often as you can. You never know what might be the next big thing, and it's always better to ride the wave, rather than letting the wave crash down on you one day. Hindsight is the worst. You always wish you had gotten into something, or bought that stock when it was pennies, but it's normally too late. So don't just sit there, learn everything you can about any industry you're interested in, and fully immerse yourself in it until you're an expert. Maybe you won't make a ton of money in the process, but at least you'll be able to educate others and eventually turn a profit that way.

I'm going to leave you with one more list (you know how much I love them). This is a summary list of everything you should do when starting a new company.

1. Find a problem in the world to solve
2. Figure out if there is a market for your idea
3. Validate your idea / run surveys
4. Research the space / industry
5. Outline your idea
6. Build as much as you can
7. Start looking for cofounders
8. Form a company
9. Create documentation
10. Give out equity
11. Begin building your MVP
12. Use SCRUM and iterate fast
13. Document everything
14. Research UI/UX
15. Work on your name / brand
16. Launch your Beta
17. Get test users
18. Gather and analyze data
19. Create a press release
20. Write blog content
21. Promote on social media platforms
22. Write up a Q & A

23. Create a promo video
24. Make data driven decisions
25. Run A/B tests
26. Learn your target market
27. Find out your key metrics
28. Use the customer acquisition funnel
29. Create the perfect pitch deck
30. Write your story and practice it
31. Write an executive summary
32. Get all your documents in order
33. Make sure you have the 4 T's
34. Find the right investors for your startup
35. Keep track of all connections you make
36. Use growth hacking tactics
37. Look for partnerships
38. Begin fundraising
39. Make sure your company is scalable
40. Learn from mistakes
41. Stay healthy and have fun
42. Listen, listen, listen
43. Never give up
44. Become an expert
45. Minimize your expenses
46. Make priority lists (like this one)
47. Set goals and reach them
48. Constantly add skills to your arsenal
49. Choose a job your love
50. It's never too late

Strap on your Boots

Congratulations! If you are reading this, you are ready to strap on your boots and plunge into the world of starting a business. I've given you all the tools that you will need in order to succeed. I've also given you plenty of examples to help you along the way. Always remember that this is a process, and it will take time. So be patient, listen, learn, and become an expert. If for any reason you still need more help, there are plenty of other resources on the Internet, or you can always reach out to me for a more personal consultation.

Enjoy the journey and your life, help others along the way, and visualize your goals. Use your creativity to build a unique company. Look for pain points in the world that could use some disruption. Get together with other creative entrepreneurs to join you on your journey. Never lose sight of your goals, and never get discouraged by roadblocks. Always strive for the positive in every situation, and take plenty of breaks along the way.

If you find yourself stuck and would like to book a private consultation with me, you can do so on my website:

https://JasonSherman.org - You'll also find a widget on my site where you can pitch your idea to me. I'll send you feedback either way. Also if you want to take what you learned in this book to the next level, I suggest you enroll in my class on Udemy.com - it's called Startup Essentials, and here's a shortcut link: http://Class.JasonSherman.org

And if you are looking for daily inspiration and more great information, then feel free to subscribe to my iTunes Podcast at: http://Podcast.JasonSherman.org

I wish you the best of luck, and hope you succeed in achieving every goal you have in life!

\<About the Author/\>

Jason Sherman is a serial entrepreneur, award winning filmmaker, journalist and tech startup expert. He has been featured by many media outlets such as *the Wall Street Journal, USA Today, The Verge, and ABC News*. He is fluent in Spanish, is a classically trained violinist, and was a featured speaker on *FOX's* Emmy Award Winning Futurist TV Show: *Xploration Earth 2050*.

Jason runs a technology consulting company and film studio from Philadelphia, Pennsylvania. He gives guest lectures at top universities, and teaches a class based on this book at the University of Pennsylvania's Wharton School of Business. His methodologies on entrepreneurship and data driven decisions are his main source of education to those he helps all around the world. Visit him online: JasonSherman.org